Left Wing, Right Wing, People, and Power

The Core Dynamics of Political Action

Douglas Giles

Real Clear Philosophy

Text and graphics copyright © 2024

All Rights Reserved. No part of this publication may be reproduced, stored in a retrieval system, or transmitted, in any form or by any means, electronic, mechanical, photocopying, recording, or otherwise, without prior permission of the Publisher.

ISBN: 978-1-7358808-3-9

Real Clear Philosophy

Contents

1. What Are "Left Wing" and "Right Wing?"	1
2. What Is the Core of Politics?	9
3. A Brief History of the Right Wing	19
4. Two Liberals—One Right and One Left	29
5. The Spectrum of Left Wing and Right Wing	37
6. Right-Wing Movements Today	55
7. Left-Wing Movements Today	68
Appendix 1. The Fake Left	79
Appendix 2. The Fake Political Dimension	86
Forward Foreword	96
Bibliography	99

1. What Are "Left Wing" and "Right Wing?"

Politics is usually portrayed as a contest or battle between politicians. This is ironic because what the word "politics" really should mean is a sense of community.

The word "politics" comes from the ancient Greek word "polis," which simply means "the city." Ancient Greek society was based on the city-state, so politics, the affairs of the city, relates to all things political and applies to all things about the city or society. From the word "polis" we get the idea of politics, the idea of police, and the idea of the suffix of a city in words like "metropolis."

Politics is the discussion or debate about how government and society should be structured, how decisions for society should be made, and how social institutions should function and to what ends. There are multiple forms of government and many ideas about how society should work, but all are subject to decision-making, and decision-making is subject to those who have the power and status to influence decisions and the social institutions that enact decisions.

At its core, all politics is about power—the power to make and manifest decisions. That includes political power, certainly, but power is an issue in all dimensions of social life. The discussions about government and society revolve around questions about who has power, how power can be exercised, and how it can be abused.

Discussions about the nature of political power have been going on for a very long time. Plato warned against the abuses of political power 2,300 years ago. He condemned the unrestrained power of a tyrant—an absolute ruler. Plato's opposition to tyranny included opposing democracy as a form of government and decision-making because he thought it was too prone to abuses of power.

Plato reasoned that humans in a democracy seek personal advantage over others. Opposing factions emerge and struggle for power, and democracy can "promote [to leadership] anyone who merely call[s] himself the people's friend."[1] Plato feared that someone with enough charisma and guile would grab power by securing the loyalty of enough voters. Once in power, the politician could become a tyrant and suppress those who might challenge the tyrant's power.

Plato's alternative, outlined in his book, *Republic*, was to grant political power to a small class of people he called "guardians," who would be highly trained to make rational decisions for the benefit of society as a whole. Concentrating power in the hands of a talented elite few would, he reasoned, ensure an ideal ordered society.

History has shown that the political formula of a concentration of power has been enacted many times, though most often lacking Plato's concern to train those in power to make decisions that benefit society. Key questions pertinent to any society are who has power, how they are using their power, and for whose benefit that power is used.

Left/Liberal and Right/Conservative

Politics is complex, befitting the complex issues faced by every society and the myriad complex solutions people offer to address those issues. To simplify politics, political parties, politicians, and people in general reach for terminological shorthands. It's common practice to describe parties, people, and political positions as being Left or Right—liberal or conservative. But are these labels accurate? What do they mean?

The words "liberal" and "conservative" each have a broad set of meanings outside of political contexts. To be "liberal" or "conservative" is acting positively or negatively relative to the situation, and most of the meanings of those actions are not related to politics. For example, one can be "too liberal" or "too conservative" with one's estimates or applications of ingredients.

---

[1] Plato, *Republic*, trans. Desmond Lee (Penguin, 2007), VIII.558.

Uses of "liberal" and "conservative" in political contexts are fairly recent developments. According to the *Merriam-Webster* dictionary, the English words "liberal" and "conservative" were first used as nouns in a political sense in 1814 and 1831, respectively.[2] The *Merriam-Webster* basic definition of being politically conservative is to adhere to traditional, established forms or ways, and its basic definition of being politically liberal is to be willing to depart from those forms or ways. These are incomplete definitions, but they are good starting points.

Edmund Burke, a philosopher and politician in the late 1700s in England, predated the term "conservative" but with good reason is considered the founder of political conservatism. Writing in 1790, Burke argued, in essence, that established, traditional values, forms, and ways have withstood the test of time.[3] They therefore should be respected and not allowed to be undermined by speculative innovation or passions. He didn't mean that we should never question or change established forms or ways but that we should not do so lightly. We'll explore Burke's conservative political philosophy in Chapter 3.

The political use of the term "liberal" is more complicated. One general use means to be more open-minded to new ideas in contradistinction to conservatives, but the other usage, ironically, is quite the opposite. We'll discuss this contradiction in depth later in Chapter 4.

Commonly associated with the political use of "liberal" is the term "left wing," which first appeared in English in 1844.[4] Complementarily, the political use of "conservative" is associated with the term "right wing," first appearing in English

---

[2] *Merriam-Webster.com Dictionary*, s.v. "liberal," accessed February 2, 2024, https://www.merriam-webster.com/dictionary/liberal. *Merriam-Webster.com Dictionary*, s.v. "conservative," accessed February 2, 2024, https://www.merriam-webster.com/dictionary/conservative.
[3] Edmund Burke, *Reflections on the Revolution in France* (Oxford University Press, 2009).
[4] *Merriam-Webster.com Dictionary*, s.v. "left wing," accessed February 2, 2024, https://www.merriam-webster.com/dictionary/left-wing.

in 1856.[5] "Left" and "Right," unlike "liberal" and "conservative," are words specifically related to politics, having originated as descriptions of political action.

The earliest uses of "left wing" and "right wing" in politics did not reflect political philosophies or ideologies. Instead, they indicated support for or opposition to a particular government. "Left wing" and "right wing" as relative terms came from their first uses in the midst of the French Revolution.

Beginning in 1789 in the National Constituent Assembly, supporters of the king chose to group themselves sitting to the right of the assembly speaker, and opponents of the king sat opposite them on the left. The French newspapers of the time used the terms "the Left" and "the Right" to describe the opposing sides, and this use spread throughout Europe.[6] Before long, political movements opposed to a sitting government were called "the Left," with "the Right" referring to those who supported that government.

Edmund Burke was an influential voice in opposition to the French Revolution that overthrew the established monarchy. Burke's argument against the Revolution was not blind reactionism to change but a well-considered philosophical critique. Fundamentally, he accused the revolutionaries of failing to appreciate and understand the historical development of ideas about social conduct and relations of power that had supported government. Burke argued that the revolutionaries' passion for the idea of liberty for all failed to grasp that liberty was only one power among many necessary for a civilized society. Liberty is a power, and giving power to the masses would sweep away the refinement of ideas that had developed through many years and created institutions like the monarchy that benefited society.

---

[5] *Merriam-Webster.com Dictionary*, s.v. "right wing," accessed February 2, 2024, https://www.merriam-webster.com/dictionary/right-wing.

[6] Jeremy D. Popkin, *A Short History of the French Revolution*, 7th ed. (Routledge, 2019), 92.

Mary Wollstonecraft, a contemporary of Burke in England, was of exactly the opposite opinion from him about the French Revolution. Also writing in 1790, Wollstonecraft saw the French Revolution as a necessary rational response to the corruption of the French absolutist monarchy.[7] She embraced the new ideals of progress and social reform, in particular the idea that women should be equal to men. Wollstonecraft took the view that all humans, regardless of their social class, have natural, God-given rights. She therefore condemned the tradition of hereditary privilege and the inequalities of the class system and social structure that kept power in the hands of the upper class. Social institutions that denied natural rights needed to be swept away, she argued. Government should extend freedom and the other God-given rights to all people regardless of sex or class.

Burke's and Wollstonecraft's contrasting positions on the French Revolution exemplified the basic perspectives on politics and power that we now call "Left" and "Right." These basic perspectives predate Burke and Wollstonecraft, though these two thinkers sharpened the focus on what is at stake in political conflict. Two centuries later, we are still debating the same basic perspectives in the arguments sparked by the French Revolution, of which Burke and Wollstonecraft were only a part.

But what realities are behind the labels "Left" and "Right?" When we refer to, for example, the right wing or right-wingers, to what are we referring? What does it mean for someone to be a left-winger or a right-winger? We use these labels to signify political positions and actions, but what do these political positions mean?

The media, politicians, and even philosophers, don't adequately examine the meaning of "left wing" and "right wing." We are all so used to these terms that we hear and use them without a second thought as to their meaning. Many

---

[7] Mary Wollstonecraft, *A Vindication of the Rights of Woman and A Vindication of the Rights of Men* (Oxford University Press, 2009).

political conflicts have considerable effects on our lives. We deserve and need a deeper understanding of politics and political action, and we can help accomplish this by having clearer understandings of terms and that to which they refer. In this book, I want to clarify the meaning of the terms "left wing" and "right wing" in ways that help us better understand political and social conflicts.

What "Left Wing" and "Right Wing" Don't Mean

For a start, politics is not "red team" versus "blue team." The corporate news media, whose bread and butter are stories about conflict, portray politics as a sports contest. The media talking heads opine on who they think is currently winning the messaging battle between the Left and the Right, who is scoring more points against the other side. The media engages in little analysis of actual political issues or how those issues affect people. The portrayal of politics as a spectator sport, exacerbated by social media shout fests, has reduced the idea of the political left wing and right wing to a simplistic oppositional binary.

We see this dynamic of binary opposition in the squabbling between the supposedly left-wing Democratic Party and the supposedly right-wing Republican Party in the United States. The policy differences between the two parties are much smaller than their rhetoric would have us believe. What differences they have cannot be reduced to the caricatures of big-government liberals versus small-government conservatives, especially because both of those labels are deeply ambiguous, and neither party consistently fits into them. Substantial discussions of political issues are all but forgotten as both parties seem more interested in scoring points against each other, and the corporate media is more interested in keeping score.

Today, "left wing" and "right wing" have become such generic terms that they are empty of meaning beyond a vague sense that they are opposites. The unthinking use of these terms mischaracterizes most political parties and movements. Some of that mischaracterization is by design, with "left wing" and "right-wing" being used pejoratively. The Left and Right caricature each other. Political rhetoric at times crosses into political propaganda attempting to demonize the other side as being too extreme Left or too extreme Right.

Too often, the right wing casts left-wingers as irrational, uncivil rabble-rousers or worse—dangerous antisocial miscreants. Left-wing political parties are at best chastised as being against common sense but usually are castigated as dangerous subversives out to dismantle social institutions.

Too often, the left wing denounces right-wingers as ignorant hotheads who are either openly or tacitly bigoted. Right-wing political parties are at best chastised as being against civil liberties but are often condemned as fascists out to demolish social institutions.

There are also the less caustic stereotypes of the bleeding-heart liberal and cold-hearted conservative. Stories are told that the Left is too soft to get anything done and the Right is too harsh to be allowed in government. These stereotypes are less incendiary than the outright insults, but they still are caricatures that serve only to demean and demonize opponents.

The drive to define left wing and right wing in terms of mutual opposition extends to how people define themselves. The terms "left wing" and "leftist" are used by many as shorthand for their opposition to the rich and powerful. Many of those who take on the label "leftist" use it as an expression of hostility to the right wing rather than as an indicator of the ideas they support. Does being a leftist mean anything more than hostility toward those who have more power than you?

The words "right wing" and "conservative" are adopted by many to express the desire to conserve the status quo, meaning opposition to reforms. That is what the term "conservative" meant to Edmund Burke, but what the status quo is in any given time and place is relative to circumstances. Do "conservative values" mean something beyond resistance to change? Those who identify as being from the Right use the term more as a synonym for their feelings of moral superiority over the supposed miscreants on the Left than as an indicator of the ideas they support. A recent example is the right wing's adamant "antiwoke" posture, although they have difficulty defining "antiwoke" beyond it being a synonym for "anti-Left."

Do "left wing" and "right wing" mean anything other than "not Right" and "not Left?" Yes, and no, as we will explore in this book. The rhetoric from political parties and the media doesn't tell us what left-wingers and right-wingers actually believe other than that both sides feel their side is correct and the other side is wrong. But correct at what? What is the motive for all of the opposition in politics? Are there core meanings to being left wing or right wing?

For a term to be useful, it needs to reflect a tangible concept. To call anything "Left," "left wing," or "liberal" has meaning only when and if we know what "left wing" means. The same goes for the terms "Right," "right wing," and "conservative." Rather than mindlessly reuse the same terms over and over, let's analyze the left–right divide and try to understand what's going on.

Again, politics is not "red team" versus "blue team." True, part of politics is opposition, and political action is agonistic. Political parties stress their distinctions from other parties. But political actions have goals beyond simply attacking one's political opponents, though you could be forgiven for thinking otherwise. People and parties get involved in politics to accomplish political goals. By exploring what those goals are, we can identify the real points of contention between two different visions for society. We can then come to a clearer understanding of "left wing" and "right wing."

2. What Is the Core of Politics?

Pulling back the curtain on political rhetoric, we can start to see what's really going on in politics. What are people trying to accomplish when they engage in political action, and what is their motivation? One help toward answering these questions is philosopher Leo Strauss's seminal essay entitled, "What Is Political Philosophy?"[8]

Strauss lays down two particularly important ways of looking at what is political. One is that he observes that all political actions aim at either preservation of existing political circumstances or changes to existing political circumstances:

> All political action aims at either preservation or change. When desiring to preserve, we wish to prevent a change to the worse; when desiring to change, we wish to bring about something better. All political action is, then, guided by some thought of better or worse.[9]

Strauss is here identifying a central, if not *the* central, dynamic of political action—people desiring change for the better in tension with people desiring to prevent change for the worse. This dynamic tension over whether change should or should not happen provides much of the agonistic character of politics.

As Strauss also adeptly points out, political activity is dependent on the idea of the good:

> ... thought of better or worse implies thought of the good. The awareness of the good which guides all our actions, has the character of opinion: it is no longer questioned but, on reflection, it proves to be questionable. ... All political action has then in itself a directedness towards knowledge of the good: of the good life, or the good society.[10]

People who participate in politics, however they are involved, are all guided by a sense of what they believe is the ethical

---

[8] Leo Strauss, "What Is Political Philosophy?" *The Journal of Politics* 19, no. 3 (1957), 343.
[9] Strauss, 343.
[10] Strauss, 343.

good. That sense of the good is what motivates their political actions. However, though people believe they have knowledge of what the good is, it is often the case that, on reflection, their view is questionable—it is simply their opinion.[11]

Politics almost invariably comes down to disagreement over whether what is good (or at least better) for society is achieved through either changing or preserving existing political circumstances. Political disagreements are so often hostile because the opinion about whether preservation or change is the better option is passionate but saturated with imperfect understandings. Even when political conflict descends into yelling among political opponents, the reality is that people on both sides of the shouting match believe that what they are trying to do is good—ethically good and even ethically necessary.

The dynamic of preservation versus change is central to political action. Perhaps some people prefer preservation or change for their own sakes, but most are taking their political positions because they believe that the tangible political actions that they support will lead to good outcomes. Also common in political actions that aim at either preservation or change is that achieving those aims depends very much on who possesses greater power to bring about their desired ends.

The Importance of Power

We can identify another constant factor among all instances of political actions, a factor consistent with Strauss's view of political actions as either preservation or change motivated by the concept of the good. That factor is power—social, political, and economic power. Despite specific differences of time and place, political actions are consistently efforts to preserve or change the dynamics of power and who possesses power in a society or community.

---

[11] For an overview of Leo Strauss's political philosophy, see Catherine R. Zuckert and Michael P. Zuckert, *Leo Strauss and the Problem of Political Philosophy* (University of Chicago Press, 2014).

There is certainly the question of what power actually *is*. There are so many manifestations of power, and so many avenues through which power can circulate, that we need a thick and robust conception of power rather than a simplistic definition. Our concept of power needs to be able to identify and evaluate the motivations of political actions.

Byung-Chul Han, in his 2018 book, *What Is Power?*, observes that people typically think of power as "the power of the *ego* ... which effects a particular behaviour in [another person] against the latter's will."[12] From Niccolò Machiavelli[13] to Max Weber[14] to Michel Foucault,[15] political theorists predominantly have viewed power as coercion and discipline, a force by which a person or institution causes others to act in a certain way by overcoming or neutralizing another person's will. This conception of power as a battle of wills is also widely held by people beyond philosophy, as is long evidenced in history. Nevertheless, this conception is too simplistic. Social reality is far more complex.

Han expands the concept of power beyond coercive acts that repress others' wills. Power manifests on a continuum, Han says, a scale of the intensity of mediation—communication—among people.[16] Violence and freedom are the two end points on Han's scale of power. Where mediation is

---

[12] Byung-Chul Han, *What Is Power?* (John Wiley and Sons, 2018), 1. (emphasis Han's).

[13] Machiavelli, neither in *The Prince*, trans. George Bull (Penguin, 2003) nor in the *Discourses on Livy*, trans. Julia Conaway Bondanella and Peter Bondanella (Oxford University Press, 1997), offers an explicit definition of power, but it is fair to assess that he held that power was the ability to, by whatever means necessary, impose one's will on others.

[14] "[Power is] to realize their own will in a communal action even against the resistance of others." Max Weber, "Class, Status and Party," *Essays from Max Weber*. H. H. Gerth and C. Wright Mills, eds. (Routledge, 1948).

[15] "Power is essentially that which represses." Michel Foucault, *Society Must Be Defended*, trans. David Macey (Macmillan, 2003), 15. It can be argued that in his later writings, Foucault broadened his conception of power, but power as coercion, punishment, and repression was the predominant conception in his oeuvre.

[16] Han, 5.

reduced to nil, power turns into coercive violence, and people relate antagonistically to each other. When the intensity of mediation increases—when there is a flow of constructive communication—power enables freedom.

Between these two end points, or extremes, on the scale of mediation of power, we find the myriad power relations among people. Power does sometimes manifest as coercion and repression, but power also manifests in positive ways and in communications and actions between the constructive and the coercive. Individuals sometimes act to coerce others, but they also act to develop and express themselves and their freedom.

To understand political action, we need to take into account techniques of domination and techniques of the self because, as Han observes, people use power to construct their own senses of self and freedom. As Nythamar de Oliveira observes, acts of domination of individuals over one another involve processes by which the individual constructs the self.[17] How an individual forms a sense of self and expresses himself or herself socially is part of the political dynamic of how individuals attempt to preserve or change the dynamics of power.

Axel Honneth argued that receiving recognition from others is a condition for an individual's self-realization, including how an individual responds to political and social injustices.[18] Honneth is correct about the human need for mutual recognition, but I agree with Danielle Petherbridge who countered that Honneth's theory of struggles for recognition fails largely because he does not include an adequate account of power.[19] I previously offered my own critique and expansion of

---

[17] Nythamar de Oliveira, "Affirmative Action, Recognition, Self-Respect: Axel Honneth and the Phenomenological Deficit of Critical Theory," in *Justice and Recognition* (Filosophia and PUCRS, 2015), 69.

[18] Axel Honneth, *The Struggle for Recognition: The Moral Grammar of Social Conflicts* (Polity, 2003).

[19] Danielle Petherbridge, *The Critical Theory of Axel Honneth* (Lexington Books, 2013), 92–93.

Honneth's theory of recognition[20] and here will adopt the important insight that individuals' need for recognition from others is a prime motivation for political action and use of power.

Han is correct that power is integral in forming one's own freedom within social interactions. Power creates social spaces for the ego so people can freely be with others. This insight into power and why people use power is crucial in understanding political action. Han writes that "all forms of power aim at the constitution of continuity" of the self.[21] In other words, one uses power to extend oneself and manifest one's own decisions and preferences into social space and onto others. A simple example is when one tries to convince another to do something. One could use coercion or one could use gentle persuasion, but either way it is a use of power to extend one's desires outside oneself. Even something as simple as a request to pass the salt is an expression of power, albeit on a small scale.

In this way, all power is self-centric, with "self" understood as an individual human being within, not separate from, a society and place. A fundamental trait of power is acting to go beyond oneself, occupying more social space with the self. For our current purposes, we can acknowledge that when one communicates or acts, one is expanding oneself into social space and expressing one's power.

We must acknowledge that, sometimes, people's attempts to construct their own senses of self and freedom can transform into coercion of others. Nevertheless, Han's perspective helps us see that power is not simply a matter of altering another person's behavior or will. Even the most altruistic acts are expressions of power—highly mediated power that takes others into account. Power can inhibit and destroy, but power can also reduce violence though the mutual sharing of social spaces.

---

[20] Douglas Giles, *Rethinking Misrecognition and Struggles for Recognition* (Insert Philosophy, 2020).
[21] Han, 17.

All political and social actions are dependent on possessing power. One needs power whether one wants to be malevolent or do good in the world. Power is needed to invade another country or feed the poor. Acquiring, retaining, and using power is central to politics. This is true regardless of how we specifically define power. Another significant issue is the structure of power relations.

The Importance of Structure

Every person lives within a social space shaped by social institutions and norms that directly and indirectly inform people as to what they are able and allowed to do. The structure of the social space has significant effects on individuals' efforts to express and act on their desires, which is why power is central to politics and social life. Individual people seek to express and expand their power in the social space around them so that they become able to express more and do more in their lives.

We are, of course, talking about freedom—specifically, how much freedom individuals have. Isaiah Berlin identified two senses of freedom (he used the words "liberty" and "freedom" synonymously[22]). There is the negative sense, which is freedom from coercion and interference that restricts one's options. Then there is positive freedom, which is one's desire to be self-directed and the author of one's own actions. Berlin observed that there is a strong relationship between negative and positive freedoms but that the political development of these freedoms has led to these two notions of freedom coming into direct conflict with each other.[23] We will see how these two senses of freedom are viewed differently by the left wing and the right wing. But first, we need further discussion of the structure of power.

---

[22] "Freedom" and "liberty" are synonyms in the English language. "Freedom" is related to the German word "Freiheit," and "liberty" is related to the Latin word "liberte."

[23] Isaiah Berlin, "Two Concepts of Liberty," in *Four Essays on Liberty* (Oxford University Press, 1969).

Power structures—social institutions and norms—both hinder and enhance individual freedoms. Invariably, power is not evenly circulated among all the people in society. The structures of social institutions and the norms that govern their activities will affect the freedoms of different groups of people within a society differently.[24]

It is impossible for every single person within a society to have complete freedom to do everything that person desires. This reality leads to political tensions and conflicts. People undertake political action to affect the power structure to increase their freedoms, either to reduce restrictions on them or to increase their sense of control over their actions. For reasons both benevolent and nefarious, those with the power to affect the social and political power structures do so with the intent to increase or decrease the freedom and power of certain groups.

Within power structures, there are two types of power—hard power and soft power. Joseph S. Nye, Jr., defines power as the ability to obtain preferred outcomes by means of hard power, which involves actions of coercion and payment, or by means of soft power, which involves actions of attraction and persuasion.[25]

Nye, like most scholars on hard power and soft power, considers them in the context of foreign policy and international relations. However, we can also consider hard power and soft power in the context of a nation's internal politics and social relations. Hard power is the control of land and economic resources, including money and personnel, and the capacity to enact and enforce policies. Soft power is the capacity to affect social recognition norms and relations and people's perceptions and interests.

---

[24] Anthony Giddens, *The Constitution of Society* (Polity, 1984).
[25] Joseph S. Nye, Jr., *The Future of Power* (Public Affairs, 2011); Joseph S. Nye, "Soft Power: The Evolution of a Concept," *Journal of Political Power*, 14:1, 2021.

Hard power and soft power are inextricably intertwined in human society. For example, a marginalized minority group is deprived of both hard and soft (economic and social) power—seldom, if ever, only one or the other. Economic power gives one social power, and hard power enables soft power. The combination of the relations of hard power and soft power constitutes society's power structure.

Central to a nation's politics is the structure of power relations and the shares of power among various groups. Regarding these dimensions of power, we can think of two end points on a spectrum of political power structures. One end point is a structure in which power in a society is concentrated into one person or small assembly of persons. The other end point is power uniformly shared among all groups and individuals within a society.

The end point of extreme concentration of power had a notable advocate in philosopher Thomas Hobbes. In the mid-1600s, he argued that for the good of the nation, all power should be concentrated in one man, the sovereign.[26] Writing in a time of political turmoil in his native England, Hobbes proposed that to gain peace and security, citizens should agree to give up all of their individual rights and confer those rights to the absolute sovereign. The sovereign becomes the embodiment of the nation, the will of all people concentrated into one person. Possessing all power, the sovereign guides and protects the nation from internal and external threats, and the sovereign provides the coercive power that compels citizens to obey the law. What Hobbes proposed was a power structure in which citizens sacrifice freedom to gain the good of security.

Hobbes's proposal has become known as "absolutism," an idea inspired by the absolute concentration of power that the kings of France accumulated in the 1600s. Absolutism rejects possibilities for mediation because it closes the link between citizens and the absolute sovereign. People have no say in how their nation is run.

---

[26] Thomas Hobbes, *Leviathan* (Penguin, 2017).

Absolutism was the power structure in France for quite some time, as from 1610 to 1774 successive kings Louis XIII, Louis XIV, and Louis XV held near total power. The perceived stability of power was admired by some, including Hobbes, but the concentration of power was detested by many within France who were deprived of power by this political structure. The French absolute monarchy was eventually overthrown by the French Revolution when French citizens sought radical transformation of the nation's power structure.

As mentioned, the modern conceptions of left wing and right wing developed at this time, the last decade of the 1700s and the early 1800s. The French Revolution unfolded in stages of taking away absolute power from the king and circulating it more broadly. Political thinking and political actions during and inspired by the French Revolution invariably revolved around issues of conserving or changing the then current power structures of nations.

The French Revolution upending of the French power structure was earth-shattering to Europeans in a way that is difficult for us to comprehend today. In Europe, the idea and reality of rule by a single hereditary sovereign had been the norm for a very long time, an arrangement that was usually presumed to have divine sanction. The feudal power structure of sovereign, nobles, and serfs was deeply embedded in tradition and custom.

The radical idea of the revolutionaries in France was that the entire structure of power in the nation could be dismantled and replaced. They advocated for political and social reforms tending toward increasing individual rights and civil liberties. For France, it did not end well. From 1789 to 1799, France careened through mob violence, multiple coups and purges, and internal and external wars, and then Napoleon seized power in 1799, becoming an absolute sovereign.

The lasting influence of the French Revolution was that it inspired the formation of two broad political philosophies, left wing and right wing, that diverged in their opinions about power structures. Two centuries later, those basic approaches to power structures have evolved into a thorny tangle of ideas. We can understand what "left wing" and "right wing" mean by clarifying the core principles that gave each their early forms and the thoughts and emotions that continue to energize people. That requires a brief history of both worldviews.

3. A Brief History of the Right Wing

The French National Constituent Assembly members who, in 1789, sat to the right of the assembly speaker, were united by a common cause to maintain the position of the king, Louis XVI. On the one hand, their politics was a continuation of an old order that had been in place for centuries. On the other hand, their politics was a response to new events unfolding in their nation. Out of a blend of old ideas and new realities was crafted the philosophy of conservatism, the precursor to the various movements today that can be classified as right wing.

There are three main trajectories of right-wing thought—conservatism, reactionism, and libertarianism. They are at times starkly different, but they share a fundamental belief about how power should be structured. I will discuss reactionism and libertarianism later, but first, I will address the philosophy that preceded the other two—conservatism.

The Precursor to Conservatism

Edmund Burke is widely regarded as the father of conservative thought because of his philosophical attack on the French Revolution. He was English, but he sympathized with the French right-wingers and their cause. Burke was no absolutist, though. As a member of the British Parliament, he supported laws to curtail the power of the British king. His concerns were to conserve what he saw as the proper political power structure and the validity of the status and hierarchy of the aristocracy.

In *Reflections on the Revolution in France*, Burke condemned the French revolutionaries' attempts to tear down the old traditional power structure of monarchy and nobility and replace it with a new power structure of their own design. Burke responded that no single generation has the right to destroy what has been built by many previous generations. He advocated for a power structure in which rulers are responsive to the views and needs of their subjects and to the reality of social change but remain firmly connected to tradition. The proper way to address change, Burke argued, is to apply the values embodied in tradition to new circumstances. A nation's traditions are the repository of civilization, the source of ethical life, and the arbiter even of reason itself.

Unlike Hobbes, Burke did not advocate for power to be concentrated in a single sovereign but called for a slightly broader power structure resting in the aristocracy. Burke's claim was that the aristocratic institutional system of prescriptive rights and customs had grown out of a process cultivated by learned men of the past. We should thus, with devotion akin to religion, he said, revere this product of generations of collective intelligence and adapt the aristocratic structure to present circumstances. We should, he insisted, presume in favor of any settled scheme of government against any untried project because we have long existed and flourished within traditional methods and institutions.

The revolutionaries' demand for a new power structure horrified Burke, especially because of the violent manner in which they were trying to achieve it. Burke believed in citizens' political involvement, but in the context of a body politic that delineates social ranks. A social hierarchy, he thought, was necessary for the wiser to be able to enlighten the weaker and less knowledgeable. He saw democracy as a dangerous abstract rule by mere numbers. A nation and its decision-making must be guided by the responsible rule of a hereditary aristocracy. Institutions can and should change and grow, but only in response to tangible social needs, never because of novel ideas or desires, and change should happen only gradually within the spirit of the nation's living tradition.

The Burkean Worldview

Burke's rebuttal to the revolutionaries' demands for changes in the power structure set the philosophical tone for the right-wing worldview regarding change.[27] Central to the

---

[27] For a study of conservative appropriation of Burke's ideas, see Emily Jones, *Edmund Burke and the Invention of Modern Conservatism, 1830-1914:*

conservative worldview is the preference for traditional structures of power and social norms. Conservatism includes, if not requires, a resistance to principles outside of and especially contrary to established traditions and cultural realities.

The conservative worldview motivates people to political actions that seek to conserve what they consider to be tried and tested traditions that are good for society. It rests on what Burke considered the latent wisdom of prejudice—the customary judgments that have accumulated over the generations. In this context, prejudice is not bigotry, though it may degenerate into it. Prejudice is a pre-judgment—the attitude that the truth has already been found, the answer has already been given, there is no need to discuss it further.

Also inherent to the worldview of Burkean conservatism is the notion that communities are held together by an acceptance of membership and duty to the community. Independent thinking and acting are potentially contrary to community. Unity comes from one feeling that one has a place in the community even though it be but a lowly one. Being a member of a community, and being a citizen of a nation, obligates one to carry the moral burdens that one's status traditionally imposes. According to John Gray,

> conservatism's fundamental insight is that persons' identities cannot be matters of choice, but are conferred on them by their unchosen histories, so that what is most essential about them is ... what is most accidental. The conservative vision is that people will come to value the privileges of choice ...

An Intellectual History (Oxford University Press, 2017). Jones argues that conservatism wasn't invented by Burke but was developed by later British politicians and theorists who cited Burke as their inspiration. Jones is correct, but it still leaves Burke and his ideas as the master spirit of conservatism, demonstrating that very Burkean view that conservatism adapts to circumstances to craft narratives that conserve the traditional status of the upper class.

when they see how much in their lives must always remain unchosen.[28]

Conservatism's insight reflected the traditional feudal power structure of sovereign, nobles, and serfs. It is certainly the case that one's freedom of choice is limited by life circumstances, but conservatism gives a rational justification for an attitude of resignation to circumstances. Burkean conservatism has a tendency toward quietism, of knowing one's social place and acquiescing to it.

In all fairness, Burke placed the moral burden of accepting one's unchosen history firmly on the upper class, not just on the lower classes. Clearly, the aristocracy was more privileged than the working classes, but with that privilege came the obligation to use one's position in service of the community and nation. The good of the nation was what was important, and this was the good that all classes should serve.

Burke stated that rulers needed to take into consideration the interests of the citizenry, but he considered interests as belonging, not to individuals, but to social groups such as the merchant class and the landowner class. The primary social group is the nation itself. An elected representative to government, Burke said, represents not the interests of a geographical area but of the common good of the nation. Burke insisted that a representative in Parliament, of which he was one, should not be bound to the interests and inclinations of individual constituencies because "government and legislation are matters of reason and judgment, and not of inclination."[29]

It could be said that Burke and those who followed his ideas about the social hierarchy were guilty of falling on the wrong side of the is-ought problem. Philosopher David Hume, writing in the mid-1700s, identified the is-ought problem by

---

[28] John Gray, *Gray's Anatomy: Selected Writings* (Penguin, 2010), 159.
[29] Edmund Burke, "Speech to the Electors of Bristol," *The Works of the Right Honourable Edmund Burke*, ed. Henry G. Bohn, University of Chicago Press. Accessed February 16, 2024, http://press-pubs.uchicago.edu/founders/documents/v1ch13s7.html.

separating empirical realities from value judgments.[30] Hume stated that we cannot argue from descriptive statements of what is to prescriptive statements of what ought to be. Our ethical judgments cannot legitimately be derived from observation of how things are in the world. How things are may not be how things ought to be.

Contrary to Hume's admonition, because conservatism places its faith in tradition as received wisdom, conservatism is inclined to accept what is as what ought to be. If the power structure has been in place for generations, then it must be a good system and we should conserve it. The Burkean worldview accepts the values embodied in tradition and the need to consent to one's unchosen history, one's place in society. Conservatism accepts as a good and natural state of affairs the traditional existence of a two-tiered society of the haves and have-nots. In practice, conservatism was and is a rejection of proposed changes to the power structure of a two-tiered society, appealing to the presence of tradition as the ethical justification for the rejection.

The Federalists

When the American colonies fought a war seeking secession from the Kingdom of Great Britain in the 1770s, Burke largely approved. For Burke, the American revolt was fundamentally different from the later French Revolution, and this difference speaks to the heart of conservative thinking. Whereas the French revolutionaries wanted to dismantle the old power structure and replace it, the American rebels sought a much less radical restructuring. Burke saw the colonies' revolt not as a radical innovation but as a restoration of the rights and privileges of the wealthy class in those colonies.[31] He had for the same reason approved of England's so-called Glorious

---

[30] David Hume, *A Treatise of Human Nature* (Penguin, 1986).
[31] For analysis of Burke's thinking about the American colonies, see Daniel O'Neill, *Edmund Burke and the Conservative Logic of Empire* (University of California Press, 2016) and Bruce Mazlish, "The Conservative Revolution of Edmund Burke," *The Review of Politics* 20, no. 1. 1958.

Revolution of 1688 that had replaced the legitimate sovereign, King James II, with one more agreeable to the interests of the aristocracy.

The Federalists in the newly formed United States were a group of wealthy landowners and merchants who supported the American War of Independence. They were secessionists who thought that King George III and the British Parliament had too much power over the colonies, sidelining and ignoring their interests. Most Federalists were antimonarchists, not just opposed to George III's method of rule, but against the idea of a political structure of a single sovereign.

After the colonies won the war and gained independence, the Federalists as a political faction advocated for, and largely achieved, a political structure for the new country in which a federal government united the former colonies under its general sovereignty. States maintained some autonomy but were not sovereign states. Importantly, the new government would not be headed by a hereditary monarch. Equally important, the new government would be representative of the geographical territories of the states, though the representatives would be selected by the upper class, similar to Burke's ideal. The Federalists were aristocrats in all but name and wanted to increase the power of their class, not the power of the "lower" classes.

Leaders of the Federalist faction were Alexander Hamilton, John Jay, and James Madison, who later left the Federalists. As political thinkers, they wrote the Federalist Papers, published in 85 volumes in 1787 and 1788.[32] In those publications, they argued for a central government of sufficient strength to safeguard the good of the nation. Their primary topic in the papers was a detailed defense of the provisions of the new US Constitution, aiming to persuade voters in the states to ratify the Constitution. A common secondary topic was

---

[32] Federalist Papers: Primary Documents in American History. Library of Congress. Accessed February 2, 2024. https://guides.loc.gov/federalist-papers/text-1-10.

to warn against the dangers from foreign intervention, dissent among the states, and domestic insurrection. Consistent throughout the Federalist Papers was the conservative idea that power should be held primarily by a central government. As described by John Jay in the "Federalist No.2" publication,

> Nothing is more certain than the indispensable necessity of government, and it is equally undeniable, that whenever and however it is instituted, the people must cede to it some of their natural rights in order to vest it with requisite powers.[33]

On the one hand, the American experiment of founding a new nation was novel; on the other hand, it was conservative in that its innovations were grounded in valuing traditional power structures.

Like Burke, the Federalists believed that the wealthy class was more capable of ruling the nation, and thus they rejected democracy, widespread suffrage, and open elections. Forming a political party, the Federalists were a dominant force in Congress and advanced a legislative agenda based on their conservative principles. Most notably, they passed the Alien and Sedition Acts in 1798 that restricted freedom of speech and freedom of the press, ostensibly to protect the nation from enemies.

Consistently, the Federalists, as political thinkers and a political party, advocated for federal power over state government and for policies that favored banks, manufacturers, and protectionism of American business. During the Federalist era—the first years of the United States as a nation, 1789 to 1800—the Federalists consciously attempted to establish a new tradition for the new country. Their vision was a social power structure based on conservative principles of tradition and hierarchical power applied to the circumstances of the new nation. It is no surprise that Burke did not object. The

---

[33] John Jay, "Federalist No. 2" in Federalist Papers: Primary Documents in American History. Library of Congress. Accessed February 2, 2024. https://guides.loc.gov/federalist-papers/text-1-10.

Federalist Party fell into the minority after the election of 1800, but their legacy of conservatism remains foundational to the United States and continues to affect the country to this day.

The Right Hegelians

The events of the French Revolution were a catalyst for a great deal of philosophical discussion in Europe. There were those who were inspired by the idea of the revolutionaries, and there were those, like Burke, who were repelled by the prospect of the overthrow of existing traditions and institutions.

The most influential continental European philosopher who defended traditional power structures was Georg Wilhelm Friedrich Hegel, writing in the first two decades of the 1800s.[34] Hegel's philosophy was broad and obscure, easily interpreted in various ways as philosophers took what they liked from his ideas. Interpretations of Hegel's political philosophy fell into two camps—the Left Hegelians and the Right Hegelians, reflecting how they applied Hegel's insights into a left-wing or right-wing view of political power structures. The most famous of the Left Hegelians are Friedrich Engels and Karl Marx, who transformed Hegel's ideas into forms with which Hegel would never have agreed. None of the Right Hegelians ever reached individual prominence; this camp was more of a general movement more conducive to Hegel's philosophical system that influenced later German political philosophy.

Foundational to Hegel's political philosophy is his notion of historicism. For Hegel, the history of the world and society is to be understood as the working of an objective, rational order. Hegel observed that we can understand events only after they occur. Human reason and freedom are historical achievements, each generation dependent on earlier ones. Only through studying supposedly objective history can we know ourselves

---

[34] Georg Wilhelm Friedrich Hegel, *Elements of the Philosophy of Right*, ed. Allen W. Wood, trans. H.B. Nisbet (Cambridge University Press, 1991). Georg Wilhelm Friedrich Hegel, *Political Writings*, ed. Laurence Dickey and H. B. Nisbet. (Cambridge University Press, 1999).

and understand how the nation should be structured. For Hegel, rationally realizing one's role as a cog in the machine of history is the realization of freedom, and the fullest realization of freedom is understanding one's role in the political nation-state.

Hegel did not advocate absolutism as Hobbes had. Instead, Hegel called for a constitutional monarchy—the rule of a sovereign possessing power but bound to the law of the constitution that expressed the interests of the aristocracy. All institutions and individuals are to obey the *Sittlichkeit*, the ethical order. For Hegel, *Sittlichkeit* is "ethical behavior grounded in custom and tradition and developed through habit and imitation in accordance with the objective laws of the community."[35]

Hegel's historicist system is clearly a defense of the nation and its existing power structures. In that, it is a right-wing political philosophy. In Hegel's view, the nation is the result of a rationally ordered system of historical development. The power of the nation is its *Sittlichkeit*, which provides the parameters of human rights and freedoms. Individuals can think and act freely, but only within the parameters of the ethical order.

Hegel's insight that freedom exists within the framework of an ethical order is profound and clearly accurate. It's an insight that has significantly inspired philosophy and the social sciences—in particular, clarifying the need to see the rule of law as the means for both positive and negative freedoms. The right-wing interpretation of Hegel's philosophy extended the notions of historical inevitability and a hierarchical rational order as the basis of the social power structure. Right Hegelians also emulated Hegel's strong strain of nationalism and the idea of German society as superior, a bulwark to radicalism.

This chapter is by no means an exhaustive account of right-wing thought. It serves as a background for the assertions

---

[35] Hegel, *Phenomenology of Spirit* (Motilal Banarsidass Publishers, 1998), 266.

made and actions taken today by adherents of right-wing ideas. Conservatism is in essence the standpoint that what is ought to be because it proven tradition. It is skeptical of novel ideas to change existing power structures. Conservatism's worldview puts trust instead in heritage and the social hierarchy.

4. Two Liberals—One Right and One Left

Conservatism is the politics of conserving the power of tradition and existing power structures. Burke, the Federalists, and Hegel couched politics in terms of freedom, or liberty, for some in society. Again, the terms "freedom" and "liberty" are synonymous, but different thinkers and movements use one over the other. In this chapter, because it discusses two different political movements using the term "liberal," I will use the word "liberty."

Regardless of which term is preferred, prominent in politics and political theory are the issues of power and freedom. They are actually the same issues, because, as Byung-Chul Han points out, power and freedom are not opposed to one another but are manifestations of the one power.[36] People wish to maintain and/or expand their power and the liberty to exercise their power.

Here, we pick up the discussion of Isaiah Berlin's two senses of liberty—positive and negative.[37] Negative liberties are the absence of forces that restrict the options available to you, usually understood as liberty from coercion—negative in the sense that there is no repression of your liberty to act. Positive liberties are the ability to act on available options and the power to effect changes that one wants in the world—positive in the sense that one has the power to act. Berlin showed that negative and positive freedoms can be rival, incompatible interpretations of a political ideal, both interpretations claiming the words "liberty," "liberal," and "liberalism."

It is impossible for every single person within a society to have complete liberty to do everything they desire. Nevertheless, liberties can be either restricted to specific social groups or expanded to more social groups. The French Revolution was a demand that liberty—and power—be expanded beyond the privileged upper class to the lower

---

[36] Han, 17.
[37] Berlin, "Two Concepts of Liberty," in *Four Essays on Liberty* (Oxford University Press, 1969).

classes. Conservatism as a political philosophy grew out of an opposition, not to liberty and personal freedoms themselves, but to the idea that expanding liberties required the destruction of existing power structures. Conservatism seeks literally to conserve power as it is already structured.

The tensions between these two competing desires—expanding liberty and conserving liberty—is a major element of politics. In competition are struggles for the power to act with liberty (positive liberty) and struggles for the liberty to act with power (negative liberty). These struggles can be compatible because power and liberty can be complementary. However, power structures that benefit some groups more than others circulate power and liberty unequally, stimulating different groups to have different political agendas; some groups focus on negative liberties, and some groups focus on positive liberties. These different agendas seeking different liberties create political tensions.

These tensions over liberty define much of the conflict between left wing and right wing. The term "liberal," of course, derives from the term "liberty," but it is incorrect to define "left wing" and "right wing" in terms of one being in favor of and one being opposed to liberty. Both the Left and the Right justifiably claim liberty as a value they defend, but there are decided differences in their views on what liberty means and who should have liberty.

To illustrate the nature of the left wing and the right wing, we need to distinguish between two quite different uses of the term "liberal." Both uses derived from historical attempts to increase liberty. In these historical contexts, both the left wing and the right wing used the term "liberal" accurately in the trajectory of their political goals. Over the centuries, one political trajectory that has used "liberal" has strayed far from increasing liberty, and its continued use of "liberal" is mistaken if not deliberately misleading. This is the right-wing political movement using the term "libertarian." In sharp distinction are those political movements called "liberal" that are left-wing.

Why these two groups are so different comes down to how their historical trajectories focused on increasing either negative liberties or positive liberties.

Increasing Negative Liberties

One use of "liberal" is by those who focus on increasing negative liberties, calling for a realm of personal autonomy from which the state is legally excluded. This trajectory has its roots in the late 1600s when the aristocratic class of England sought more autonomy from the monarchy. The 1688 Glorious Revolution was so named by its instigators—a group of English aristocrats—who replaced the legitimate sovereign, King James II, with one more agreeable to their interests. It was not a revolution but a political coup, and its rebranding was an example of history being written by the victors.[38]

Philosopher John Locke wrote *Two Treatises of Government*[39] in 1689 to justify philosophically the coup in which he had been involved. Locke's basic argument is that government is a convenience. It is not necessary, and it is not divinely ordained. Rational people established government because they find it preferable to live in an ordered society based on law rather than in anarchy. Locke viewed government as a social contract between the people and the government, with the people saying, "we appoint you to rule as long as you serve our interests." If the sovereign, or government in general, breaks the terms of the social contract, they have lost any right to remain in government. The people have the right to replace them.

Whether Locke would have approved of the American War of Independence we can't say for certain, but the new nation of the United States found inspiration in Locke's philosophy of a division of powers—checks and balances—in

---

[38] Steven Pincus, *1688: The First Modern Revolution* (Yale University Press, 2009).
[39] John Locke, *Locke: Two Treatises of Government* (Cambridge University Press, 1988).

government. The Federalists blended Locke's ideas with Burke's traditionalism to create a constitution that delineated the power structure of government. Locke would have approved of the new US government divided into multiple branches of power, with all members of government decided by members of the upper class.

Locke advocated a right to disobedience of authority, but he was not an anarchist. He believed in ethics and laws and that people should obey authority to keep the peace within a society. The rule of law and a strong, concentrated political structure must be maintained, Locke said, to defend people against anarchy. The Federalists agreed with this position. People did not have a right to revolt against their sovereign government except in the face of egregious tyranny from that government.

The libertarian trajectory of right-wing thinking has focused on the right to revolt against tyranny. In the early United States, a political viewpoint arose more extreme than the antimonarchism of the Federalists. This faction, colloquially dubbed the "antifederalists," opposed the idea of a constitution and a federal government, preferring instead a social power structure in which power was wielded by local owners of land and business.[40] The American penchant for individualism, buttressed by the westward expansion increasing the availability of land and natural resources, fed the libertarian trajectory of thinking that the structure of power should be shifted from government to the wealthy class.

By the last half of the 1900s, libertarianism, largely in response to the emergence of corporatism (global capitalism), came to target any government as an enemy to liberty that must be eliminated. Today, this involves using the term "liberal" in its narrow focus on particular negative liberties, defining "the state" and any of its possible actions as coercion and interference that restrict an individual's options for action.

---

[40] Jackson Turner Main, *The Antifederalists: Critics of the Constitution, 1781-1788* (Omohundro Institute of Early American History and Culture and the University of North Carolina Press, 2017).

Movements with this view of liberty include economic liberalism, libertarianism, neoliberalism, anarcho-capitalism, and anarchism.

Despite the use of the term "liberal," these views are based on a simplistic interpretation of "the state" as inherently tyrannical. In the name of increasing negative liberties, the libertarian trajectory seeks to remove power from government, which, they claim, will lead to an ideal society of greater negative liberty.

People holding to the libertarian use of "liberal" are, in reality, of the right wing. The libertarians seek to conserve a power structure ruled by an economic aristocracy. Unlike the conservatives, the Federalists, and the Right Hegelians, libertarians reject governmental authority. The libertarian trajectory has been the ideology of some wealthy individuals and corporations attempting to concentrate power in their hands by eliminating the rule of law that could hold their use of power to account. The libertarian ideology has been expressed by theorists such as Ludwig von Mises,[41] Murray Rothbard,[42] David Friedman,[43] Robert Nozick,[44] and David Fraser Nolan.[45]

Increasing Positive Liberties

Although a strain of liberal thought focused on positive liberties can be traced back as far as Desiderius Erasmus in the 1400s, the other use of "liberal" associated with increasing positive liberties arose in the 1700s. This trajectory came not from the aristocracy but from other elements of society. These people advocated increasing positive liberties for the majority, not just for the aristocracy. This trajectory of thinking that can

---

[41] Ludwig von Mises, *Liberty & Property* (Ludwig von Mises Institute, 2018). Ludwig von Mises, *Human Action* (Ludwig von Mises Institute, 2009).
[42] Murray Rothbard, *For a New Liberty: The Libertarian Manifesto* (Ludwig von Mises Institute, 2010).
[43] David Friedman, *The Machinery of Freedom: Guide to a Radical Capitalism* (Chu Hartley, 2014).
[44] Robert Nozick, *Anarchy, State, and Utopia* (Blackwell, 1974).
[45] Founder of the Libertarian Party in the United States.

correctly be called "liberalism" in contrast to conservatism encompasses two different approaches.

One approach was a view of liberty most exemplified in Jean-Jacques Rousseau's concept of the greater common good. In this view, positive liberty is what is good for society as a whole, even when that sacrifices the liberty and well-being of some individuals. Rousseau's idea, as explained in his 1762 book *The Social Contract*,[46] was that a new power structure in which each individual is required to participate in decision-making will yield the general will of the community. When the government is directed by the general will, it reflects the interests of the people as a whole, not the interests of just a few. Thus constituted, the state can protect the people, providing them with justice and with opportunities and support in pursuing positive liberties, leading to the good for the community.

Rousseau's concept of the general will was implemented in the early years of the French Revolution but was beset by multiple ambiguities and difficulties.[47] Rousseau said that individuals are free to pursue their own desires, as long as they continue to obey the general will, but he was unclear on where individual freedom ended and the sovereignty of the general will began. It was also unclear who decided what the general will of the people was. The French revolutionaries' efforts to replace the stable, though tyrannical, old power structure with Rousseau's inherently unstable power structure contributed to the revolution's failure, a criticism correctly made by Burke and Hegel.

The other approach to increasing positive liberties aims to cultivate individuals' ability to make their own choices and empower individuals to act on their choices. This view values individual autonomy as a good for society. Liberals who take

---

[46] Jean-Jacques Rousseau, *Of The Social Contract and Other Political Writings*, ed., Christopher Bertram, trans., Quintin Hoare (Penguin, 2012).

[47] Holger Ross Lauritsen and Mikkel Thorup, eds., *Rousseau and Revolution* (Continuum, 2011).

this approach oppose tyranny, but unlike the libertarians, they see a role for government and other social institutions in promoting and guaranteeing individual liberties and power. Different from right-wingers, liberals advocate increasing positive liberties across all members of society regardless of social or economic class.

Advocates for positive liberties focus on the idea of individual autonomy—the power to be one's own person and live according to one's own reasons and motives. Left Hegelian philosopher Thomas Hill Green stated that one is free only if one is self-directed or autonomous, self-consciously responsible for one's actions.[48] John Stuart Mill was deeply concerned with negative liberty from unnecessary restrictions on individual behavior because he emphasized autonomy as a social good. Individual autonomy is essential to one's well-being and, thus, to society as a whole.[49] Therefore, Mill advocated for a government that empowered a culture of autonomy. Like Burke, Mill supported representative government, but unlike Burke, Mill thought that it was good for individuals to have democratic participation in electing their representatives in government.[50] He supported women's suffrage and expanding political and economic power to women.

Political philosophy and movements have always been driven more by opposing tyranny and aggression than by cultivating positive liberties. A good reason for this is that it seems, for the most part, that positive liberties are assertible only after negative liberties from coercion have been achieved.

---

[48] Thomas Hill Green, *Prolegomena to Ethics*, ed., D. Brink (Clarendon Press, 2003).

[49] John Stuart Mill, *On Liberty, Utilitarianism, and Other Essays* (Oxford University Press, 2015).

[50] Mill consistently wanted to expand the voting franchise beyond the upper class, but he fell short of embracing universal suffrage, preferring that voting be weighted so that those with "superior knowledge and cultivation" would have a greater number of votes. "Thoughts on Parliamentary Reform" in *On Liberty, Utilitarianism, and Other Essays*.

Positive liberties are often a still and small voice amid the louder angrier voices demanding freedom from tyranny.

Despite making the necessary distinction between libertarianism and liberalism, the terms "liberal" and "left wing" need to be defined with more depth and precision. What does increasing positive freedoms across society entail, and how does one approach this task? Answering these questions will lead us to an understanding of what the left wing is. The key distinction between liberal and libertarian conceptions of liberty is the scope of the liberties they seek to establish and defend. By making that distinction clear, we can clearly perceive the core differences in the worldviews of the left wing and the right wing, which will go a long way in helping us understand political and social conflicts.

5. The Spectrum of Left Wing and Right Wing

The Left–Right political spectrum is a common reference point in political conversation. What constitutes the spectrum remains insufficiently discussed and inadequately defined. The Left–Right political spectrum reflects political realities, and political movements and groups can be placed meaningfully along that spectrum. However, any such classifications are meaningful only if we have a clear definition of the meanings of "Left" and "Right" grounded in identifiable social phenomena. To understand what "Left" and "Right" mean, we need to look at political and social realities and avoid the distortions of political dogmas.

Chapter 2 introduced several insightful concepts about power. Chapters 3 and 4 then looked at brief histories of how the concepts of conservatism and liberalism developed. Now, we turn to building a robust definition of "left wing" and "right wing" and how these worldviews are at odds with each other. The core difference between the left wing and the right wing is which power structures they believe will achieve the good in society. Applying some basic theoretical and historical insights will make this distinction apparent.

We took from Leo Strauss the insight that all political actions aim at either preservation of existing political circumstances or changes to existing political circumstances. To accomplish even basic social tasks requires power; therefore, politics is about attaining or preserving power in the social environment. To be able to take political action requires power, especially to be able to succeed in one's political aims.

Also from Strauss, we took the insight that politics is the clash of opinions over what is good for society, a clash that almost invariably comes down to disagreement over whether that good (or at least better) is achieved through either changing or preserving existing political circumstances. The dynamic of preservation versus change is central to political action.

We took from Byung-Chul Han the insight that power manifests in a complex array of reciprocal interdependencies among people. This connects with Axel Honneth's concept that the need for people to receive recognition from others permeates all political struggles in which people seek to expand their power and freedom. Han says that people can express and expand their power through coercion and violence, which avoids mediation with others, or without coercion and violence, being open to mediation with others. The latter, he says, creates a bridge and a bond between self and other.[51] The concept of recognition as described by Honneth fits with the idea of a bond between people. Mutual recognition generates power relations that empower people to act socially and politically.

We also saw that a society has a structure of power relations among its members and between people and the government. Preserving or changing the existing interdependent relations of power is the core activity of politics. People and institutions within the power structure use hard power and soft power to attain their preferred outcomes, and the relations of hard power and soft power constitute the society's power structure.

In Strauss's terminology, people struggle over the power to produce or prevent change in the existing circumstances. In Han's terminology, people struggle for the power to express and expand themselves and their opportunities. We will see how these two concepts intertwine and combine in political actions from both the left wing and the right wing.

In short, politics is about power, and power is delineated by a social power structure of institutions and norms. The left wing and the right wing have fundamentally different preferences for power structures. That difference can be understood as a continuum or spectrum of power concentrations in the social power structure. To begin to understand this political spectrum, we need to understand

---

[51] Han, 76, 81.

power relations because the political spectrum is a spectrum of beliefs about power relations.

Power Relations and the Flow of Power

A society is composed of individual people and social institutions. The myriad relationships and interactions among people and institutions form constellations of connections and power relations. Each individual occupies a social space within constellations, and no one is completely separate from or unaffected by his or her social environment and connections.

Any particular social connection between individuals has a dynamic power relation that defines the relationship. For example, an employer and employee, members of a family, friends, teacher and student, and a citizen and a governmental institution all involve a power relation. The power relation is dynamic in that it can be altered by external circumstances or the actions of participants.

Power relations between individuals can be understood as occurring on a spectrum from dominance to mutuality. Some interpersonal relations are more mutually beneficial when one person has more power, such as teacher–student and parent–child relations. As long as power is not wielded maliciously or without proper regard, the person with less power in the relationship will benefit from the mentoring he or she receives. For most relationships, such as friendships, people receive greater benefits when they share power more equally. If in a personal relationship one person has too much power, that relationship is unhealthy.

In society's larger constellation of relationships, there are dynamic power relations similar to those in interpersonal relationships. These include power relations between institutions and individuals. The nature of relations between institutions and individuals means that these power relations are weighted such that institutions wield more power. Some of these relationships are more beneficial when the institution has more power than the individuals, such as a school and its students. Here, too, as long as power is not wielded maliciously or without proper regard, individuals with less power in the relationship will benefit from the power relation. However, there is a high potential for abuses of power by institutions over individuals, which is the case whenever and wherever power is weighted too heavily to one side of the relationship.

Given that a society is composed of myriad relationships, each one with a power relation, many relationships are largely defined by the power relation between the participants. The entire social constellation of relations of people and institutions composes the society as a whole. The government and the predominant culture form the society's core power structure in which the myriad constellations of social relationships play out.

Each nation or society has its social, political, and economic powers structured in a particular arrangement. To understand a society's politics and its citizens' quality of life, we can ask which people and which institutions possess power and to what degree. Power structures affect people and their quality of life because those power structures both hinder and enhance people's freedoms. The dynamic of power relations and people attempting to conserve or change power relations plays out within the society's power structure.

Power structures unevenly affect different groups of people, producing different effects on their freedoms. Social institutions do not evenly share power, leaving some people to have more power than others. Inequalities of power are a common cause of political action as people seek to change what they perceive as unjust absences of power.

It is generally the case that there are inequalities of power. There are a number of possible reasons for inequalities of power, from differences in levels of individual talent or effort to structural inequalities that prevent individuals from benefiting from their talents and efforts.

Power is not a commodity like food or raw materials; nevertheless, power is something that people can gain, exchange, and use in their social relations. Certain individuals can, through their own actions, attain greater power. For example, individuals can earn greater respect from their peers, or gain knowledge through experience and education, or gain more money through work or business dealings. Such a possession of power can be precarious—what one can gain one can also lose through circumstances or the lack of diligence.

Power relations are dynamic in that power can actively flow among people and institutions within social constellations, and power relations can change. In an open society with greater freedom, social institutions foster positive freedoms that enable people to exchange and use power in their social relations. A high presence of positive freedoms enables people to act to achieve their goals, change their power relations, and take advantage of opportunities to gain more power through achievement.

When positive freedoms are encouraged, people can express and expand their power in the social space around them. Power flows among people. When social institutions welcome input and involvement from people, the power relations are less coercive, and chances of malicious exercises of power are reduced. When the social power structures are open, people, through their own actions, can better or worsen their social circumstances and power relations.

Hierarchical Power Concentrations

The social power structure can also entrench possession of power and power relations, thereby hindering the exercise and flow of power. A social caste or class structure has been part of many societies, creating inequalities that are an inherent part of the society's power structure. People in a privileged class possess a higher level of social, political, and economic power. People outside of that class have less power. These class hierarchies are not always codified in the law but can be enforced by social norms. When the social power structures are stratified and entrenched, power does not flow freely within social constellations, and it is more difficult for people to better or worsen their social circumstances and power relations.

Power concentrations can be self-perpetuating because powerful families and castes have the power to maintain their power. Some individuals are fortunate enough to be born into a family with wealth and status and thus are born into a realm of greater power than others are. Families can pass their wealth and power to their descendants, perpetuating concentrations of economic if not political power. These fortunate ones naturally have a vested interest in maintaining their power and privilege and in defending against change of the prevailing power structure that facilitates their power. Obviously, this is not a given—power can always be lost, but it is a truism that having power better enables one to have power in the future.

Jacques Rancière is correct that society will always have a social order in which there are inequalities, but there are better and worse orders.[52] Taking that fact into account, if we want to understand how hierarchical class structures can be harmful, we need to look at the aspect of power relations that is power concentration. When a power structure inherently benefits one class over others, it is concentrating power in a small segment of society—for example, an aristocratic or business owner class. There is a definite economic component of power concentration, on which Karl Marx and like-minded thinkers focus, but economic power is as much a product of structural power concentration as it is a cause of class hierarchy. It is a chicken-and-egg conundrum of which comes first—economic power or class distinction—so it is better to acknowledge that power concentrations are a synergy of social, political, and economic power, of hard power and soft power.

When power is concentrated in a minority, power circulates only within a small number of social relations and a small sphere of social space. Concentrated power means power does not flow among people and institutions, which solidifies

---

[52] Jacques Rancière, *Disagreement: Politics and Philosophy*, trans., Julie Rose (University of Minnesota Press, 1998).

power relations and power structures across spheres of society. Such a society's institutions and norms give preference and privilege to a higher class. People in the privileged class find that the social power structure enhances their efforts to express and expand their power in the social space around them. People outside the privileged class find that their attempts to gain more power are most likely hindered by social institutions and norms.

The level of power concentration is a vital factor for a society and the people living in it. One's power is being enhanced or hindered by the social power structure, and where and how that structure concentrates power is a momentous issue for people—it affects many aspects of their lives.

A Spectrum of Power Concentration

Because the core of politics is power, the issue of power concentration is a major political issue. It is partially a question of which institutions and people possess power in a society, but it is also a question of the degree to which power is circulating among institutions and people. Inequities of power in a society are probably inevitable, and may even be beneficial, but history records that when a great deal of power is concentrated in one small group, it will be coexistent with a loss of power and freedom for those groups without power.

Whatever the amount of power within a society, there is a spectrum of power concentration. We can illustrate what concentration means in this context with the example of money—financial power. If two-thirds of the total wealth in a nation is possessed by one percent of the population, then wealth in that nation is more concentrated than in a nation in which half of the wealth is possessed by one-third of the population. In the latter nation, money is possessed and circulated more widely. Other forms of power are much more difficult to measure than monetary wealth is, but the reality of power being more or less concentrated or more or less widely circulated can be understood.

To repeat, there are two end points in the spectrum of power concentration. One end point is a structure in which all power in a society is concentrated into one entity such as a sovereign. The other end point is power uniformly shared among all groups and individuals within a society.

Both end points are more theoretical limits than realities. Human history has seen instances of near absolute concentrations of power, but one person having all power is probably impossible to achieve or maintain. The same is true of uniformly circulating power—what mechanism could exist to enforce that no one person ever has more power than another? It would seem that even attempting to attain either extreme would lead to forms of oppression negating negative liberties. Regardless, all nations and subcultures within a society have greater or lesser concentrations of power, and they can be compared with each other on a spectrum of power concentration.

A totalitarian society is one in which power is concentrated in the hands of a very few, so power is exchanged among and used by only a very few. Power can be concentrated in a government or in a group such as an aristocratic or business-owning class. Particular social institutions or particular laws can also concentrate specific powers in the hands of a few. Examples are legal and social practices of racial or ethnic segregation that concentrate power in the possession of selected groups. Structures that perpetuate gross economic inequality also concentrate economic, social, and political power in the hands of an elite few.

Here is an especially crucial point: It matters less where or in whom power is concentrated than that it *is* concentrated. What matters is the structure of power—how power is or is not shared among members of a social community. It also matters less what the size of the social community is—the fundamentals of power relations are the same regardless of scale. A totalitarian national government, a company town, an anarchic warlord or gang leader, and an oligarchic business syndicate all share the same structure of power concentrated in the hands of a few. A concentration of power necessarily means that other people are excluded from power, have less freedom, and are most likely coerced and exploited by those in power. These realities are why power concentration is the central issue of politics and the primary cause of political action.

Advocating for Greater Power Concentration

Politics is the set of debates and actions over ways to achieve the good life or the good society. To those ends, arguments have been made in favor of greater or lesser concentrations of power. First, here are some examples of the arguments for power concentration.

As mentioned earlier, Thomas Hobbes thought that concentrating power in a single sovereign is optimal for achieving the good. Hobbes considered the central issue of politics to be the issue of security, which he believed to be a social good. He believed that security could be achieved by concentrating authority in the singular sovereign. The alternative, he assumed, was the state of nature—the anarchy of life without laws or social norms, a state of being in which life was nasty, brutish, and short.

Hobbes was writing in a political and social context different from ours, one in which monarchs held great power. His formula of an extreme concentration of power was not a radical divergence from the political realities of his time. Few people, if anyone, would say they are Hobbesian today. Nevertheless, there have been a large number of voices calling for a strong concentration of power for the good of society, even if the only good sought was for a particular social group.

A more recent advocate of concentration of power was Carl Schmitt. He was primarily a legal scholar, but he published extensively on political theory. Schmitt contended that a state is capable of decisive action only if power is concentrated in a singular sovereign authority—a dictator. He saw dictatorship as essential to legitimate government, especially in times of crisis.

Schmitt saw politics as the struggle between friend and foe. It is thus incumbent upon the state to define clearly who is friend and who is foe and must be able to mobilize all available resources to defend itself and its friends from all enemies. To be successful, a state must concentrate power in the dictator, an absolute sovereign who exercises power prior to and as an exception to the law. Because Schmitt believed that politics is fundamentally a struggle against enemies of the state, he believed that the state needs to be in an almost continual state of exception (*Ausnahmezustand*)—a crisis mode in which constitutional law is suspended and the dictator rules by fiat, an exception to the law, ostensibly in the interests of the good of the state.

As an unapologetic fascist, even before the rise of the Nazis, Schmitt advocated for dictatorship in multiple books (*Politische Romantik*, 1919; *Die Diktatur*,[53] 1921; and *Politische Theologie*,[54] 1922). In 1934, he published, *Der Führer schützt das Recht* (*The Leader Protects the Law*) in which he linked the notion of a sovereign power that is above the law with the person Adolf Hitler. He was a passionate member of the Nazi Party and openly anti-Jewish. He used his positions as a professor at the University of Berlin and in the Nazi regime to call for a purge of all Jewish ideas and influences in German academia and the law.[55] Until his death, he never repented of his support of Nazism and its extreme concentration of power. It is not surprising that Schmitt's ideas have found favor from Russia's Vladimir Putin and China's Xi Jinping.

Hobbes and Schmitt both believed that the good could be achieved by concentrating power in a singular sovereign authority. We can see that their position on power was a more extreme version of the concentration of power advocated by conservatives such as Burke, the Federalists, and the Right

---

[53] Carl Schmitt, *Dictatorship*, trans., Michael Hoelzl and Graham Ward (Polity, 2013).
[54] Carl Schmitt, *Political Theology*, trans. George Schwab (University of Chicago Press, 2006).
[55] Claudia Koonz, *The Nazi Conscience* (Belknap Press, 2005).

Hegelians. The right-wing political viewpoint is that greater good will be attained by greater concentrations of power in a smaller segment of society. This was true of Hobbes and his idea of the sovereign, of Burke and the Federalists and their ideas of the wealthy class ruling the nation, the Right Hegelians' belief in the necessity of a hierarchical rational order, and Schmitt's call for dictatorship. These are prominent examples of a strong tradition in political thinking that calls for a greater concentration of power. All of these calls are expressions of the right wing of the political spectrum.

Power Concentration Versus Power Circulation

Human history has been marked by struggles for power to be more widely circulated. I mean this not in terms of simplistic Marxist ideology of the alleged necessity of the working class wresting power from the bourgeois class but in terms of the reality of many different people seeking greater social, economic, and political power for themselves. The core of politics is the disagreement over how power should be structured, and it is a struggle with more dimensions than Marx's vision of a dualistic class struggle over the means of economic production.

Throughout history, some people have tried to grab power for themselves and have attempted to establish concentrated, exclusive power structures at the expense of others. Other people have attempted to change prevailing political structures, striving to open up the circulation of power to a greater number of people. These rebellious movements have been struggles for social liberties, political recognition, and material resources.

What connects all of these conflicts is that they are ultimately over the circulation of power versus the concentration of power. The particular circumstances were relative to time and place, but they were all conflicts between those who wanted power to be concentrated in fewer people and institutions versus those who wanted power to be shared by more people and institutions.

These struggles over power relations characterize the left-wing–right-wing conflict and the political spectrum. Is power widely circulated or narrowly concentrated? Is a political movement seeking to increase or to restrict the circulation of power?

Answering these questions defines the left wing and the right wing and enables us to understand the motives for political actions. Social and political structures that concentrate power into a small number of people or institutions are right-wing structures. Right-wing movements are characterized by their desire and efforts to concentrate power more. In contradistinction, social and political structures that circulate power among a large number of people or institutions are left-wing structures. Left-wing movements are characterized by their desire and efforts to increase the circulation of power.

The circulation of power is when power relations are not entrenched in a hierarchal power structure but are open for people to gain or lose power through their actions. A dictatorship is an extreme concentration of power in a single sovereign. An oligarchy is less extreme, but still a concentration of power in a minority class. If such power structures are dismantled, people previously outside of the structures are literally empowered to claim greater participation and freedoms in society. Such a society is a more open society in which people can alter power relations by their personal choices and actions. A society with a robust circulation of power doesn't guarantee that every individual will have power, but it has fewer impediments to people being able to express and expand their power in the social space around them.

"Left wing" and "right wing" are terms that are most informative when they describe someone's goals as to the general direction of power concentration and circulation.

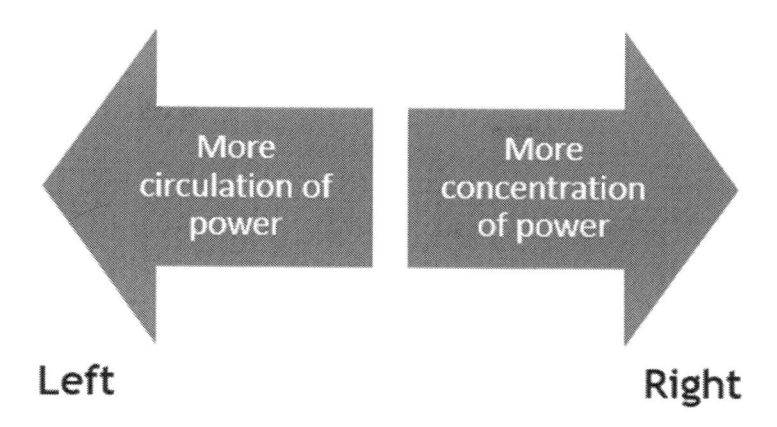

Left ← More circulation of power | More concentration of power → **Right**

The greater a society's social and political structures concentrate power, the more right-wing that society is. The more a society circulates power among its citizens, the more left-wing it is. Civil rights struggles for legal recognition are leftist because they seek increased equality for oppressed minorities—in other words, greater power for those who are disempowered by the prevailing power structure. Feminism, for example, is left-wing in its objective to end power being concentrated in men and change social institutions so that power is more circulated to include women. Conversely, anti-immigrant, antifeminist, or white supremacist movements are right-wing movements that seek a return to more exclusive concentrations of power.

Labeling these movements as "left wing" and "right wing" is independent of any moral judgments about the proponents' intentions. All of these groups would see their particular causes as ethically just; they are seeking what is, in their opinion, the ethical good. Sincere, intelligent discussions can be had about whether particular circumstances warrant a greater or lesser concentration of power.

Applying the Power Spectrum

Understanding "left wing" and "right wing" as a spectrum of power concentration gives us a clear approach that can be applied to any social situation. This approach empowers us to understand where an individual or group is on the political spectrum by assessing political power structures and people's political opinions, motivations, and actions on the basis of what structure of power they are trying to achieve. Because we are looking at structures of power relations common in all human societies, this approach also allows us to compare political movements in different times and places. Our study of politics becomes more fruitful by focusing on social dynamics more fundamental than particular political positions, which are relative to time and circumstances and often are transitory positions.

To date, the political spectrum has largely been used as a tool of rhetoric and propaganda. All sides have been guilty in this. The rhetoric has led to numerous confusions about political positions and conflicts. Applying the understanding of the political spectrum as a power spectrum clears up common misunderstandings about politics.

One misunderstanding of the Left–Right political spectrum is that the Left–Right political conflict is the rights of individuals (right wing) versus the force of the government (left wing). This bromide is often accompanied by the myth that the Left is about state control of the economy and the Right is about economic freedom. These portrayals are a right-wing polemic that inaccurately equates the left wing's quest to expand the circulation of individual power with statist authoritarianism. It is true that governments have had to intervene to protect the rights of minorities, but to castigate, as the right wing does, these interventions as governmental overreach or even as tyranny is an unabashed declaration that it is wrong to extend rights and power to minorities. Often, the caricatures of small-government conservatives opposing big-government liberals are used to restrict power to a few and preserve structures of inequality.

The actual issue is not the size of the government but the effectiveness of government in facilitating human freedom and prosperity. Unless one takes the extreme opinion that there is no role for government in society, it seems self-evident that government's role is to defend the rights and freedoms of citizens from those who seek to deprive others of them. Who is against the basic concepts of rights and freedom? No one. Nevertheless, some people *are* against granting rights and freedom to particular other people. It has long been established that a legitimate role of governmental power is to protect the powerless from exploitation and abuse and to provide for the general welfare. This notion predates any modern conception of "liberalism" and is found in feudal and ancient societies that by today's standards would be considered despotic. For example, the Roman Empire, a society in which power was highly concentrated, still provided governmental relief to its poorest citizens in the form of food aid.

Another confusion about the political spectrum is caused by the received dogma in the United States that the right wing wants less government interference in individuals' lives and the left wing wants government to run people's lives. But the debate over abortion rights exposes this rhetoric as false. In its simplest terms, the debate is whether a woman should be legally permitted to or prohibited from terminating her pregnancy. Both sides of the debate seek to establish in law their position on that question. The Right seeks laws that prohibit a woman from having an abortion, and the Left seeks laws establishing a woman's right to an abortion.

The issue of abortion rights is self-evidently an issue of a woman's positive freedom to act on her own choice for her own body and life. The right-wing position is that the government *should* interfere in individuals' lives and possess the power to control women's bodies. The left-wing position is that a woman's positive freedom to control her own body should be protected from governmental interference. But these are the opposite positions that the received dogma tells us the Left and Right would take. This example is one of many that show that the traditional characterization of the Left–Right spectrum does not reflect the true conflict between the two sides on tangible issues.

The abortion rights issue shows that it is incorrect to characterize the right wing as holding the ideological position of limitations on state power. There is no greater imposition of state power than a power structure forbidding a human being from controlling his or her own body and future. The political positions of Burke, the Federalists, and the Right Hegelians show that the ideological position of the right wing is not to take power away from the state or government but is to restrict who has power within government.

A third confusion about the Left–Right spectrum concerns personal freedoms. Laws restricting free speech, freedom of religion, and so on are supported by the Right and opposed by the Left on the basis of how they change the circulation of power in society. This is why right-wingers can support some governmental intrusions into people's lives and not others and why left-wingers can support some restrictions on freedoms and not others.

For example, speech is power, and freedom of speech is a particularly consequential issue in how freely people can speak out against structures of power concentration. The principles of citizens' rights to criticize publicly and to make petition of grievances to the government are inherently left-wing principles that tend to be featured more often in more left-wing societies. True, even the most extreme right-wing party can say, with sincere conviction, that they support free speech. That is because the question is not whether speech is allowed but rather *who* should be allowed to have the power of speech. Totalitarian regimes reserve freedom of speech for those loyal to the regime—a concentration of power. Left-wing movements generally defend free speech rights for those who dissent against the status quo—a broader circulation of power.

Putting aside for the moment that left-wingers are often guilty of the all-too-common double standard as to who is allowed to criticize sitting leaders, the right wing by default seeks to restrict the power of speech to those they deem worthy, whereas the left wing generally seeks to expand free speech rights. This idea is consistent with the overall intention of the right wing to concentrate power rather than allow it to be widely circulated, which is not to say that freedom of speech is infinite.

John Stuart Mill recognized that a government could and should restrict speech that harms others because, in doing so, it protects individual freedom of speech without contradicting its principles of expanding freedoms. Mill declared that "the only purpose for which power can be rightfully exercised over any member of a civilised community, against his will, is to prevent harm to others."[56] This formula of the legitimate uses of power has come to be known as "the harm principle." Restrictions based on Mill's harm principle are expressions of left-wing principles because harmful speech disempowers and silences others and because these restrictions seek to increase the circulation of power.

Right-wing polemicists erect a straw man portraying the left wing as power-hungry statists eager to stamp out individual liberties. This caricature contradicts the fact that left-wing movements, most prominently those favoring civil rights, women's rights, and gay rights, are motivated by the desire to increase individual freedoms by increasing the circulation of power.

Left-wing polemics erect a straw man of the right wing as power-mad tyrants conspiring to torment the masses. Desiring to concentrate power is not necessarily malicious, and it is incorrect to assume that people on the Right are devoid of intelligence or compassion.

The specifics about what freedoms citizens should have involve a large, complex set of questions. We can get past unhelpful polemical rhetoric if we accept that both the left wing and the right wing see freedom as a positive good and if we see

---

[56] Mill, 13.

the difference between the left wing and the right wing in terms of concentration of power.

Understanding "left wing" and "right wing" as the conflict over the circulation or concentration of power puts the question of power where it belongs—as a primary motivation and goal of human political action. Political parties and movements seek political power to enact agendas that either further concentrate or further circulate power in society. Particular political issues are also about either further concentrating or further circulating power in particular circumstances. Who has power and how the use of power affects others are what is at stake in politics.

Accepting the centrality of power concentration in politics also demythologizes the political spectrum. Notions of a teleological struggle between The Left and The Right may be romantic, making for good press, but such stories do not reflect the realities of human society. Political conflict is far less about a clash of political ideologies than political theorists and the corporate media portray. We must remember that most people do not live their lives in terms of grand political theory; they seek better lives in terms of economic and social comfort for themselves and those they love. Some people do want power over others, but most people desire only enough power to manage their own affairs successfully. Understanding the Left–Right spectrum in terms of circulation or concentration of power better reflects how people look at and live their lives.

6. Right-Wing Movements Today

The right wing of the political spectrum contains three primary trajectories of thought and action—conservatism, libertarianism, and reactionism. The specifics of each trajectory differ, but they share a common goal—to conserve and/or return to traditional power structures that restrict power to a small group, creating a two-tiered society of the haves and have-nots. Because they share the essential goal of restricting power to a select group, they are right-wing. Because they have significantly different self-identities, and therefore engage in different political actions, they are distinct social movements.

Conservativism

Many people and groups adopt or are described by the labels "conservative" and "conservatism." The terms are familiar descriptions of ideological positions in multiple areas— fiscal conservatism, religious conservatism, and social conservatism.

I am using "conservatism" to describe people and groups following Burkean conservatism—the belief that social good is best achieved by the rule of an established upper class in which power is concentrated. Adherents of conservatism, past and present, believe that power should primarily be held by an aristocracy, in practice if not in name, which controls the government and economic power structures. Conservatism is also a rejection of proposed changes to the power structure, appealing to the presence of tradition and traditional values as the ethical justification for the rejection.

Quite sensibly, conservatism is led by members of the upper class who are the dominant sector of society. I will refer to them as the "vested conservatives" (VCs). They are people who have a high enough economic and social status that they have a vested interest in maintaining the status quo of power relations. Burke and the Federalists were VCs in their time, and there have been VCs throughout history before and since then.

For VCs, the word "conservative" has its literal meaning. They seek to conserve their concentrated social, economic, and political power and their separation from the common people. They are people who attempt to conserve current socioeconomic inequalities because those inequalities benefit them. Their social identity is grounded in a sense of their upper-class superiority to the masses. Their political positions are expressions of their desire to maintain and expand their power in the social space around them.

VCs include the über-rich and those who believe they are or should be in that upper-upper class. They insist that there be little or no regulation on business, low taxes on the wealthy and corporations, and a strong government that works for the interests of the wealthy and powerful. In the United States, the VCs seek a return to the laissez-faire America that existed before the social reforms of the 1950s and '60s and perhaps before the New Deal of the 1930s or even before the antitrust laws passed from 1890 to 1914. They are the pro-business conservatives, often calling themselves "fiscal conservatives." Their political identity is vested in a vision of government as the entity that defends the property rights of the wealthy.

The goal and purpose of political action for the VCs is controlling government so that government works for their interests. The political issue for conservatism is less about governmental power than it is about economic power. Government is a tool to further the concentration of power in the über-rich business and landowning class. Karl Marx didn't invent the idea of a class struggle. The notion that the good and natural order is a two-tiered society of the haves and have-nots existed long before capitalism emerged around the time of Edmund Burke and conservatism. Capitalism is only one manifestation of the belief that the good is achieved by power being concentrated in the über-rich who control economic power.

The VCs are right-wing in acting to influence government and the media to promote concentration of wealth and power in their small segment of society. That is their legal and ethical right. There is nothing wrong in voting for one's self-interest; that is the heart of democracy. Nor can we blame any VCs for otherwise being politically active to defend and expand their interests. Yes, the rich have the right to express their self-interest politically and have their voices heard, but the rest of us should understand their actions and political positions for what they are: They want to increase power for themselves.

Conservatism still often falls on the wrong side of the is-ought problem, in the view that those who are rich deserve to be so. This is not necessarily the case—nor is the opposite view, that the rich necessarily are that way because of unjust exploitation of others. Conservatism largely continues the traditional assumption that wealth inequalities between rich and poor are how things should be. Thus, a two-tiered society, largely divided on difference of economic power, is natural, and to oppose this traditional power structure is unnatural.

Libertarianism

At times overlapping the interests of the VCs are the right-wing libertarians. Libertarian philosopher Robert Nozick provides arguably the strongest intellectual expression of libertarian ideology.

Nozick advocates for the concept of a minimal state wherein there is minimal intervention from the state and people are entitled to economic and personal liberties. He proposes an entitlement theory of justice in which a person who acquires property in accordance with the principle of justice is entitled to that property.[57] That person has the right to hold or transfer that property to another person. In the latter case, as long as the transfer is conducted in accordance with the principle of justice, the new property holder is entitled to that property.

---

[57] Nozick, 150.

Nozick's argument is internally consistent, but what "in accordance with the principle of justice" means is debatable and easily interpreted in self-serving ways. Nozick's interpretation is that justice means the individual's right to all negative freedoms—to do as he or she wishes without any interference. He makes the extraordinary claim that any behavior is allowed as long as the individual pays market compensation for any damage caused to others.[58] Critics have pointed out that such a view favors those with greater financial resources. Nozick claims that acquisition of property creates an inviolable right of the individual to do whatever he or she wants with that property. He offers no means to correct abuses of property acquisition, only a vague suggestion that such abuses are wrong but wouldn't happen in an ideal society.

Nozick arrives at a tamer version of Hobbes's idea of the state of nature, but Nozick's is made less nasty and brutish by a "minarchist" state—a government with only minimal powers to enforce the law. A state is preferable to anarchy (the absence of all government and normative order) in that it can protect individuals' rights, mainly property and financial rights.

Nozick's book has been cemented into the foundation of libertarian political ideology. Nozick had said that the minarchist state was preferable to anarchy, but libertarianism generally prefers anarchy to the state. Libertarianism holds that individuals should have complete freedom to do whatever they want as long as they are not coercive toward others. However, most libertarians reject the idea of positive liberties ("people have a right to ..."), concentrating instead on negative liberties ("the government has no right to interfere with me"). Thus, libertarianism rejects governmental regulation of business, and extremist anarchist elements within libertarianism demand the abolition of government.

One branch of libertarianism, anarcho-capitalism, states that corporations should be allowed to create their own private

---

[58] Nozick, 75.

enforcement agencies to defend their property rights.[59] With no government oversight, power is concentrated in corporate entities. It is primarily on this issue that libertarianism differs from conservatism. They are both right-wing in the desire for a concentration of power, and they agree that power structures should favor a concentration of economic power in a business and landowning class. But whereas conservatives see government as a useful tool to this end, libertarians do not, believing, hoping, that the sheer force of concentrated power in the über-rich makes government unnecessary. Western society may already be moving past conservative capitalism and into libertarian corporatism—the power structure of rule by corporations.

As mentioned in the section on the two uses of the term "liberal," libertarianism is right-wing. Libertarianism places its faith not in tradition, as does conservatism, but in power itself, holding that there should be no legal authority to interfere with an individual's or business's exercise of power in society. Power is thus unaccountable to anything but itself. Despite its gloss of extolling liberty, libertarianism inexorably trends toward a society of domination and conflict.

For these reasons, libertarianism, like conservatism, falls on the wrong side of the is-ought problem, unquestioningly favoring the aristocratic class of whoever currently holds power in society. Libertarian ideology is a form of might makes right—a Thrasymachian view that what is ethical and logical for society are the interests of the strong.[60] This is an acceptance of what is as what ought to be. Believing that liberty comes from a power structure of strong individuals free to act without legal accountability, libertarianism, like the other trajectories of the right wing, seeks to conserve power in an aristocratic class and is skeptical of ideas to change existing power structures.

---

[59] Murray Rothbard, *For a New Liberty: The Libertarian Manifesto* (Ludwig von Mises Institute, 2010).

[60] Plato, in *Republic*, attributes to Thrasymachus the position that "justice is nothing else than the interest of the stronger." Book I, 338c.

Reactionism

The VCs of the upper class are a minority of people in any society, and the libertarians are an even smaller minority. Most right-wing people also desire the restriction of power in society, but they lack the socioeconomic status and power of the VCs. In the 1700s and 1800s, representatives to government were chosen by men in the upper class, as Burke and the Federalists wanted. Gradually, political reforms increased opportunities for people outside of a white male elite to vote for who represents them in government. Political actions in Europe and the United States to extend voting rights to more people persisted into the early 1970s, by which, at least in theory, voting rights became universal.

Nevertheless, the VC minority remains a formidable political presence in many societies because they successfully generate votes for their proxies in government. Their electoral achievements are due to various reasons, but a significant one is their success at harnessing the political power of reactionary right-wingers.

More numerous than the conservatives and libertarians, the reactionaries are people of a particular worldview—reactionism—that approves of and seeks to reaffirm previous hierarchical social divisions. The reactionaries don't possess the power of the upper class, but they perceive themselves as possessing some social privilege by dint of being the "right" ethnicity, religion, or other social identity that traditionally held a higher position in the power structure.

Over time, the world has become more connected and diverse. Minorities and women have gained more power. More people are included in the political process and in business and culture. These changes in the circulation of power are unsettling to some people, and some of those people react against them, preferring power to remain more concentrated.

Reactionism is the response to—and the reaction against—increased diversity and inclusion in society.

Reactionaries feel they are under siege and even oppressed by changing social norms and demographic shifts. Not all people who are unsettled by social change take political action to oppose those changes. Those who do take action are the right-wing block that seeks to reassert traditional, even archaic, power relations and structures. These are the reactionaries, whose political focus is on reversing the long cultural trend of increasing diversity and inclusion that has circulated more power to more people.

Corey Robin recently proposed the existence of a "reactionary mind," [61] which he defines as the hostility to emancipating the lower classes, and he argues that the reactionary mind is the central theme of the right wing since the French Revolution. There is truth in Robin's theory, but it applies to the current trajectory of reactionism and not to conservatism and libertarianism. The entire history of the right wing is not an ideology of reaction but is consistently an ideology of power concentration; there is a difference between a resistance to change to power structures and the hostility to diversity that is found in reactionism. They are different expressions of power and have different goals in power relations. This difference becomes clear when we compare the power relations that the reactionaries seek versus those that the conservatives and libertarians seek.

Conservatives and libertarians seek to conserve their own power and their own positions in the hierarchical power structure. They functionally are an aristocratic class, and their political actions are motivated by the desire to conserve their economic power, with little regard to how it affects others. Reactionaries, on the contrary, do not have a high place in the hierarchy. They may not possess any real power or wealth. Their political actions are motivated by a desire to deprive other people of social power. Reactionaries' actions are directed by their sense that what little power they have is threatened by

---

[61] For example, Corey Robin, *The Reactionary Mind* (Oxford University Press, 2011).

change and diversity and by their deeper fear of difference. This fear-driven opposition propels reactionaries to a social and political agenda to reassert a particular homogenized purity in society.

The "reactionary mind" is a fear of difference, a fear that causes the need to have others kept powerless. Reactionaries will often portray themselves as fighting in a culture war against the Left. They have an intense despair over the present social trend toward increasing diversity and equality. They contrast what they believe to be current social degradation with their image of a previous golden age. Of course, this glorified past was a time when power was concentrated in the dominant class, and many people were shut out from full participation in society. A return to this bygone era of widespread social exclusion is the ultimate goal of the reactionaries.

For example, in the United States, the reactionary agenda is a return to an America that never really was, a country where everything was "great" because the privileged status of white evangelicals was unchallenged and unhindered. Reactionaries believe that something has been lost in the United States, and they blame minorities, foreigners, feminism, and the left wing. Theirs is a vision of an imaginary pre-1960s United States—a world in which the power structure and who was good and who was evil were clearly delineated. Minorities, women, and other marginalized peoples knew their place—and if they did not, they were sharply reminded.

In their political actions, reactionaries worldwide are driven by oppositional politics—a reductionist Us-versus-Them view of the world and everyone in it. They believe that they are the "true" Americans/English/Germans/<insert ethnicity here>. They therefore demand that power be concentrated in their social group to the exclusion of all who differ. Conservatives could be said to have a positive agenda of expressing and expanding power. Reactionaries, because they are focused more on their opposition to others than on advancing a positive agenda, are fixated more on taking away power from other groups, such as minorities, immigrants, nonheteronormative people, and women. That fixation extends to hostility toward anyone in the left wing who acts to circulate more power to those groups.

Because they seek to concentrate power into their own social group to the exclusion of other social groups, reactionaries are right wing. They are emotionally opposed to progress, diversity, and civil discourse about society and power relations. The fear and anger of the reactionaries are easily manipulated and exploited by the VCs, creating reactionist political movements.

Right-Wing Alliances Falsely Labeled "Populism"

By definition, the right wing seeks to concentrate power in a small sector of society. Because the self-interest of those who are in the upper class of the power structure is to retain, express, and even expand their power, those people use their power to conserve the existing power structures and power relations that benefit them.

Concentrations of power inherently exclude certain people, which creates social and political conflict. A question that philosophers and political scientists have long pondered is how a powerful minority can get cooperation and compliance from a less powerful majority. The VCs accomplish this by taking advantage of the reactionary right wing.

In many countries, the right wing as a political force is increasingly a union of the VCs and reactionaries. The VCs have the money, and the reactionaries have the numbers, and together they exert political influence. Examples of such political parties are the Austrian Freedom Party, France's National Front, the Alternative for Germany party, Hungary's Fidesz party, the Netherlands Party for Freedom, and Poland's Law and Justice party. Major parties that were center-right, such as the UK Conservative Party and the US Republican Party, have harnessed the electoral power of the reactionaries but have found their parties all but taken over by extremist reactionary views.

Scholars and the media have labeled those present-day political parties as "populist," casting populism as an anti-elitism movement of the working class against the ruling class.[62] Agrarian movements, such as the Farmer's Alliance and the People's Party in the United States in the late 1800s, fit this loose definition in that they saw their movements as defending the working class against a dominant elitist class of exploitative industrialists and government.

Those earlier movements and parties were not economically right wing, however. Populist movements seek to shift power structures to move social boundaries and include more people in legal and social power. The right-wing parties falsely labeled "populist" do not seek to alter traditional power structures. Whatever antigovernment sentiments the current right-wing political parties have are less a matter of class antagonism than they are the belief that the government is blind to perceived external threats to society. They are reactionary movements that can be used by and even aligned with elements of the social and political elites who profess to share their opposition to diversity and inclusion. This is why wealthy elite Donald Trump can head a reactionary movement while openly pursuing economic policies that do not favor the people from whom he seeks votes. The VCs can engage in a political agenda favoring their interests while offering a message that appeals to and enhances reactionaries' sense of aggrievement and fear of the presence of "undesirables" and of social changes.

It is obvious why the wealthy want to retain a status quo that benefits them, but it takes a certain amount of subterfuge for the VCs to convince the reactionary rank-and-file voters to defend a socioeconomic power structure that is inherently against the reactionaries' own interests. The reason why this

---

[62] For example, Cas Mudde, *Populist Radical Right Parties in Europe* (Cambridge University Press, 2007).

subterfuge works is because the VCs can exploit the fundamental psychology of the right-wing mindset.

Central to the success of the VCs' agenda is to convince a large enough segment of the population to vote for candidates who will enact that agenda. This is the alliance of the VCs and the reactionaries. Money is the tail that wags the electoral dog. The enormous amounts of money that go to political campaigns and lobbying of governments are part of a deliberate effort to advance the interests and well-being of the wealthy and powerful by activating the reactionary base.

We can more easily see how this alliance forms by considering how Han's conception of power connects with Honneth's theory of recognition—the dynamic that one needs recognition to exercise social power. Others must value you and recognize your thoughts and actions as acceptable to follow your lead. As Honneth observes, even if one lacks economic power, one can still develop a strong sense of identity and belonging if one receives recognition from one's peers.[63]

This line of reasoning helps illuminate how reactionary social and political movements arise and function, especially in the online world. Winning recognition can enable a leader to exercise power through the mediation of others. One way is to convince people to draw an Us–Them distinction in such a way that the Us is the leader in opposition to the Them. The leader is therefore the power actor, and the leader's welfare is what is important. The followers receive recognition through belonging to the leader's movement, and the leader receives recognition and power through the support of the movement.

Reactionaries, feeling unsettled by social change, and disposed to thinking in terms of Us-versus-Them, find recognition in reactionary movements and parties that cater to their fears. The VCs' corporate media stoke reactionaries' fears with frenzied visions of imaginary threats from immigrants,

---

[63] Axel Honneth, *The Struggle for Recognition: The Moral Grammar of Social Conflicts* (Polity, 2003).

welfare queens, gay marriage, affirmative action, labor unions, the fictitious liberal media, liberal politicians, and government agents. The VCs' propagandists know that the xenophobia, racism, sexism, and homophobia that permeate reactionary thinking can be easily pushed into paranoia—the conviction that Them hate Us as much as Us hate Them, and Them is coming to get Us. By being a part of a reactionary movement, people can feel they are on the better side of a two-tiered society, even when they are in reality on the less powerful side of the two tiers of the power structure.

Trumpism and Brexit are only the latest manifestations of a tradition of reactionary fear that is the natural expression of Us-versus-Them dualism. In the United States, the Ku Klux Klan, the Red Scare of the 1920s, Father Coughlin, Joe McCarthy, Nixon's Southern Strategy, the militia movement, the Christian Coalition, the Tea Party movement, and MAGA are all manifestations of a simmering constant in American politics—the anger and resentment reactionaries feel toward people who are not like them. Although the concrete manifestations are slightly different, the core remains the same—a fear of and abiding loathing for anyone who does not fit the "Proper American" paradigm of a white evangelical right-winger. The promise is to "make America great again" by depriving Them of what power they have and separating the Us from the Them.

In the United Kingdom, the VCs' Brexit campaign exploited fears of immigrants and the specter of other nations within the European Union having equal rights with the United Kingdom. The Leave campaign succeeded because the VCs adeptly harnessed resentment and right wing's nostalgia for Rule Britannia and its lost empire. The message was simple: "Make Britain great again" by separating the Us from the Them, while casting their fellow Europeans as a powerful Them out to oppress the Us.

By using the media to flood the minds of reactionaries with fears, the VCs can more easily convince them to be against laws and regulations that would favor the people over the corporations and their owners. The VCs cloak their agenda in high-sounding ideology and talk of the common good, but their policies are nothing but base self-interest. The myth of American rugged individualism is the centerpiece of the ideological propaganda in the United States. It feeds reactionary resentment while serving VC interests. Myths are sold under the individualist rubric and packaged in talking points that are eagerly parroted by the VC-owned corporate media.

The VCs oppose regulation of business such as work and product safety laws, environmental laws, and so on saying they would "hurt the corporate bottom line," and they pretend that this would hurt common people. The VCs want people in mainstream America to believe that requiring corporations to be ethical and responsible somehow hurts them. The VCs push the fiction that raising taxes on rich people to fund essential infrastructure is a threat to a mythical way of life. The VCs claim to be motivated by the common good, but if they were genuinely interested in the common good, they would willingly participate in programs that protect and empower people besides themselves.

There are seemingly endless examples of right-wing efforts to concentrate social, economic, and political power in the hands of the VCs, from taxes to regulations to foreign wars. In all of their efforts to maintain a two-tiered society of haves and have-nots, the VCs engage in ideological propaganda that manipulates reactionary fears. This propaganda is a constant drumbeat in society and influences many by affirming existing resentments and fears. These two groups, the VCs and the reactionaries, combine to create and sustain an atmosphere of political hostility in which enemies are created and demagoguery poisons the political atmosphere, by design resulting in a fierce headwind against any greater circulation of power that would change the status quo.

7. Left-Wing Movements Today

The left wing of the political spectrum includes people and organizations who seek to circulate power to a greater number of people. The left wing's goal is to create a society that is more open to individuals' participation and prosperity. To accomplish that goal, the left wing attempts to change the power structure so that it reduces infringements of negative liberties and enhances opportunities for people to develop positive liberties. That means that much of what the left wing does involves political actions to counteract right-wing concentrations of power.

One factor that complicates the goal of increasing positive liberties is that every person's freedoms are necessarily limited by the reality that everyone lives within a world. The existence of other objects (you cannot walk through walls), biology and physics (you cannot fly by flapping your limbs), and especially other people who also inhabit the world (you all can't have the same parking space at the same time) restrict your ability to act and thus your freedom to do as you please. In short, reality itself is the biggest constraint on your personal power.

An answer to these problems that is available to the right wing is to assert that certain people or a certain class of people should have more power than others. A hierarchical power structure or an Us-versus-Them attitude justifies a dualism of haves and have-nots in regard to privileges and resources. As mentioned before, there are power relations in which it is beneficial to those involved for a social institution or a person to have more power than another. However, the left wing is skeptical of the need for power dynamics to be permanently unequal and is opposed to abuses of power by institutions over individuals.

Unlike the right wing, which trends toward the simplicity of concentrated hierarchical power, the left wing doesn't, indeed can't, engage in an Us-versus-Them dualism without losing its identity and its cause of achieving a greater circulation of power. The left-wing answer to the problem that people must share the world with others is not dominance but cooperation—not reinforcing existing power structures but crafting new ones. For these reasons, political action is more challenging for the left wing than it is for the right wing.

The left wing needs to confront and deal with the complexities of social reality and not try to impose on people an ideological vision of a rigidly hierarchical power structure—the type of power structure it seeks to change. Jacques Rancière put it well in stating that those who are dominated are not victims of false consciousness or ignorance but of a power structure that makes their actions invisible and voices inaudible. Those who are dominated don't need new masters to tell them what to think and do, they need to simply be allowed to speak and be heard.[64]

The Circulation of Power

Fundamentally, a left-wing agenda is empowering individuals to be able to navigate the inherent difficulties and restrictions of life so that they can live their lives as they choose, free from oppression. Yes, the right wing will use similar language, but they want to empower only their segment of society, not all of society. Left-wing actions seek to increase personal power for a broad range of people, not a select group. That definitely means reducing negative liberties—obstacles to freewill actions—but it also means transforming social structures and institutions so that they enable individuals to take advantage of opportunities to increase their positive liberties.

Perhaps foremost in circulating power is acknowledging that every person is an individual capable of thinking for themselves and making their own decisions. A significant tool of coercive power is to reduce individuals to members of a class. We do have to consider the realities of class because the

---

[64] Jacques Rancière, *The Ignorant Schoolmaster: Five Lessons in Intellectual Emancipation* (Stanford University Press, 1991), 18, 39.

traditional power structures divided people into classes, usually to then enforce a two-tiered power structure based on class. Accepting reality as how things should be or will always be is an is-ought mistake made by both right-wingers and Marxists. Both camps reduce individuals to being members of either the upper class or the working class and prioritize group identities over individuals. It is not wrong to see those classes as historical realities, but it is harmful to view the power structure as wholly determinative of society and individuals. Denying individuality and free will is a tool of oppression used to maintain concentrations of power. Circulation of power requires accepting the reality of and further potential for individuality, free will, and personal agency.

The left wing's goal is an open society that works for all people, regardless of stereotypes of class. The goal is a society that provides equality of opportunity free of discrimination caused by power being concentrated in only a small segment of society. This idea is about achieving equality of opportunities—not equality of outcomes. Outcomes can never be guaranteed because they depend on multiple factors, including the actions or nonactions of individuals to take advantage of opportunities. The structure of the power relations in society is what enables greater injustice or greater justice. A society that works for all people can do so because it has a structure that empowers all people to act on their free will responsibly.[65]

A social power structure that empowers people does not magically appear—it must be achieved, and it must be continually sustained. Such an achievement can't be imposed but must be built through dialogue and cooperative action that includes the people involved in and affected by the power structure. Only through dialogue and cooperative action—through what Han calls "mediation"—can power be noncoercive. Right-wing power dynamics trend toward

---

[65] For an overview of left-wing thought on these topics, see *American Progressivism: A Reader*, eds. Ronald J. Pestritto and William J. Atto (Lexington Books, 2008).

coercion because they are not open and deliberative—instead, power acts, and power acts onto others.

In a deliberative society, decisions must be justified, open to deliberation and discussion, and open to change when necessary. As Amy Gutmann and Dennis Thompson describe it, "Persons should be treated not merely as objects of legislation, as passive subjects to be ruled, but as autonomous agents who take part in the governance of their own society, directly or through their representatives." [66] Such a power dynamic encapsulates a circulation of power. Power flows among those who make decisions and those who deliberate about the decisions made. As Jürgen Habermas wrote, "Power corresponds to the human ability not just to act but to act in concert."[67] Power that is not concentrated in a few allows power to flow, to circulate, and to empower people and the society as a whole.

Mediation, dialogue, and cooperation are the hallmarks of the left wing. A person or group that calls itself "left wing" but expresses power through coercion is not actually left wing. As we saw earlier, the political spectrum is the spectrum of power concentration. Parts of that spectrum are the two broad paths through which power can be expressed and expanded—with or without coercion and violence. This relation exists not as an either/or but as a spectrum of how much coercion and violence are used in any particular place and relation among people.

Power relations can also be understood as a spectrum between high and low levels of openness to mediation with others. High levels of openness facilitate communication and cooperation among people. Low levels of openness slide into forms of violence, of either aggression or exclusion. All areas on this spectrum are expressions of power, the difference depending on how power is expressed and circulated.

---

[66] Amy Gutmann and Dennis Thompson, *Why Deliberative Democracy?* (Princeton University Press, 2004).
[67] Jürgen Habermas, "Hannah Arendt: On the Concept of Power," *Philosophical Political Profiles,* trans. Frederick G. Lawrence (Cambridge, 2012), 172.

Power concentrated is power that is coercive, violent, and closed to mediation and deliberation. That is the right-wing power structure. A left-wing power structure is without coercion and violence, open to mediation, communication, and deliberation. It is a power structure in which power flows and circulates among people and institutions.

If the right-wing end point of the political spectrum is an absolute concentration of power in one person, is then the left-wing end point an absolute symmetry of power among all people? The answer is no, not only because it is impossible but because an extreme equilibrium of power would mean static power relations that would hinder individual freedoms, contrary to the left wing's goal of a circulation of power. The left wing values an open society in which social institutions foster positive freedoms that enable people to freely exchange and use power in their social relations. Power relations are not static, nor should they be.

People in the left wing differ on how active governmental institutions should be in people's lives, but they agree that government does have a role in guaranteeing basic freedoms. In particular, that means a nonarbitrary form of government—the rule of law.

The Rule of Law

A key difference between right-wing and left-wing power relations is the difference between will and law. A right-wing view of power sees power residing in the will of those in power: Those with power are allowed to act as they want, with little to no accountability to others or responsibility for their actions. A left-wing view of power includes power residing in the rule of law to which all people and institutions are accountable.

In an extreme concentration of power, an absolutist monarchy or a dictatorship, power is the will of the sovereign ruler. In a conservative power structure, political decisions follow the will of the aristocratic class, though conservatism does have a respect for tradition and the rule of law. Burke and

Hegel called for constitutional forms of government, even though those governments concentrated power into the hands of a few. Reactionism is the demand that "the will of the people" override the constitution, the will of the people being unconstrained by law. Most extreme of all, libertarianism seeks a power structure in which individual will alone rules, completely without constraints or accountability. In all of these right-wing views of power, the will of the powerful trumps all else.

The rule of law is in contradistinction to the right wing's desire for rule by a select few. The rule of law is the principle of power residing in society as a whole. No one is above the law. No one is immune from responsibility to it. A constitution and established legal precedence are the standards for government and the conduct of representatives.

As Tom Bingham has written, the rule of law is the foundation of a fair and just society, is a guarantee of responsible government, and offers the best means for securing peace and cooperation among citizens.[68] People are free to act, but their actions are accountable to the law. All are equal under the law. In this power structure, power is allowed to circulate, and individuals, through their own actions, are able to better or worsen their social circumstances and power relations.

A constitutional form of government, properly constituted and exercised, is a mechanism to guard everyone's access to justice and freedom. A stable, robust power structure governed by the rule of law can provide a stable but vibrant social environment that cultivates individuals' ability to make their own choices and empower individuals to act on their choices.

The rule of law is no panacea, however. It is complex and must be tailored to a society's circumstances, needs, and constellation of power relations.[69] Establishing a constitutional

---

[68] Tom Bingham, *The Rule of Law* (Penguin, 2011).
[69] A good resource on these complexities is *The Cambridge Companion to the Rule of Law*, edited by Jens Meierhenrich and Martin Loughlin (Cambridge University Press, 2021).

form of government doesn't solve all social problems or political conflict. The rule of law provides a mechanism for solving social problems, but people need to solve the problems; the mechanism is there only to empower people to act. That mechanism must also be maintained and defended from abuse. Maintaining the rule of law and its benefits for people and society requires deliberative democracy—it requires constant dialogue, maintenance, and change. People need to be included in social institutions such that they can be involved in the social power structure. It is when people are shut out of the social power structure that power relations turn coercive and oppressive.

The rule of law is not immutable, and this means that control over who makes and enforces the law is a political issue. Steven Levitsky and Daniel Ziblatt, in their book, *How Democracies Die*, observe that constitutional democracies are broken down not by revolutions or coups but by elected governments.[70] The political conflict between right wing and left wing is played out electorally, and it is a conflict over whether power is concentrated in the possession of a few or circulated widely under the rule of law. But it is more complicated than that last sentence would imply.

Left-Wing Activism

It is natural for people today to assume that the rule of law and democratically elected representation are the norm. However, history shows that societies in which power is concentrated in a small segment of the population have been the norm. The tradition of hierarchical power structures is why some right-wingers believe structural inequalities are natural and not to be changed: It is how things are, and, as Edmund Burke argued over 230 years ago, how things are is how things should be.

---

[70] Steven Levitsky and Daniel Ziblatt, *How Democracies Die* (Crown, 2018).

A main aspect of the conflict between the left wing and the right wing is over preservation or change of existing power structures. The right wing seeks to conserve existing concentrations of power, and the left wing seeks to change existing concentrations of power. The left wing is thus characterized by its political activism. Left-wingers are struggling to increase the circulation of power in society, which means fighting the existing unjust power structures.

Out of necessity, the left wing is an active opposition to power concentrations. Of course, the right wing is essentially a resistance to the left wing's attempt to change power concentrations. The political dynamic that plays out is that the right wing is content to leave power structures in place, the left wing wants to change those power structures, and the more the left wing succeeds in changing society, the more the reactionaries fight against the changes, becoming an asset for the right wing in its attempts to reassert concentrated power structures. The left wing's inherent character of opposition to power concentration means there is the danger of it sliding into an Us-versus-Them reactionism, an issue I will address in Appendix 1.

Much of the left wing's activism is directed at governmental and economic power because the conservative upper class seeks to control government to maintain their concentrated economic power. The libertarians seek to minimize or eliminate government to maintain their concentrated economic power. Whether our current power structure is conservative, libertarian, or a mixture of the two, such concentrations of power inevitably lead to exclusion and oppression of those left without economic power.

The left-wing remedy for concentration of economic power is to create power structures that facilitate individuals' positive economic freedoms. That means thinking beyond reducing people to upper and working classes and believing in the individual's rights to be free to act economically. Such free actions include employees' collective bargaining, employee ownership of businesses, and free enterprise.

Corporate capitalism works to close down economic competition and concentrate power in large business entities, which is why corporations seek to control or muzzle government. The counter to corporate control is free enterprise, in which power structures ensure healthy competition among independent businesses and entrepreneurs. A sports match needs rules and referees to be a successful and pleasurable game. Similarly, a society's economy needs rules and referees to be able to function for the mutual benefit of both businesses and consumers. A power structure that facilitates innovation and economic activity for all people, not just for the few, is a circulation of power.

Tradition Versus Change

Cameroonian philosopher Achille Mbembe encapsulates the left wing approach when he writes that a free society must be willing to break with the repetition of perpetual sameness of tradition that has turned into necessity. [71] In particular, Mbembe took aim at the traditions of racism and colonialism. He answers them that only by confronting the closed power structures of the past can society create the conditions for an open future. By unraveling traditional concentrations of power and opening up the world through the circulation of diverse ideas and experiences, people are empowered, and, he says, humanity emerges through the process of sharing and communicating.

The harsh reality Is that the historical norm Is the presence of excessive concentrations of power and that some people prefer that power structure and the injustices it causes. Another harsh reality is that those who want to increase the circulation of power have to fight against entrenched power. The structure of the power relations in society usually favors

---

[71] Achille Mbembe, *Out of the Dark Night* (Columbia University Press, 2021), 299.

one segment of society at the expense of others, and those structures have existed for a long time. Those who benefit from having excessive power do not willingly give up that excessive power. Right-wingers understandably seek to conserve their existing privileged positions in the power structure, and their power is entrenched in the social structure, so it is relatively easy for them to maintain.

Still, it seems that the long arc of history trends toward increasing the circulation of power and that this trend has increased general levels of freedom and prosperity. It remains to be seen whether societies that circulate power under a rule of law will persist. It also should not be assumed that the current constitutional forms of government are, in practice, circulating power among the people. Power structures and power relations remain, for the most part, controlled by a small segment of the population.

The arc of history may bend toward progressively more power circulation, but only slowly. Some revolutions advance the circulation of power little, if at all. Karl Marx was correct that the French Revolution transferred power from one social class to another but still left the majority of French citizens without power. The French Revolution produced civil liberties for the bourgeois class but not for the working class.[72] The American War of Independence had a similar result. The freedoms and rights won benefited the American merchant class far more than the working and agrarian classes. Both political movements were left-wing in that they increased the circulation of power in their nations, but their effects were limited, and power remained strongly concentrated.

Change is slow, but change does come. Political history is the long story of struggles over power relations and structures. Every improvement to society has come from the diligent efforts of those who believe in the basic principle of the left

---

[72] Karl Marx, "The Eighteenth Brumaire of Louis Bonaparte," *Karl Marx: Selected Writings*, 2nd ed., edited by David McLellan (Oxford University Press, 2000).

wing—that power should be more widely circulated across society and that all of us should have positive liberties and opportunities. We owe a lot to the many brave people who have fought for left-wing causes and have increased power for more people.

Left-wingers who want to transform society so that power structures that benefit more than a select few need to be tougher than those who are maintaining structural inequalities of power. Change is difficult, and successfully increasing the circulation of power comes only after the long struggle and sacrifice of many people committed to changing the structures of society.

To succeed, that struggle must include the courage to be open to mediation, dialogue, and cooperation with those in power and with right-wingers who oppose the circulation of power. That certainly doesn't mean tolerating abuse and intolerance from the Right. It must include an openness to constructive mediation alongside a willingness to fight against unjust concentrations of power without falling into the Us-versus-Them dualism of the right wing.

Appendix 1. The Fake Left

The long and arduous process of struggling for greater circulation of power and freedom is frustrating. The reality that traditional social power structures often create injustices and oppression is angry making. It's easy, too easy, to give in to emotions of frustration, anger, and desire for vengeance. When people on the Left stray away from focusing on empowering people and instead focus on tearing others down, they move away from being left-wing into the oppositional politics of the fake Left.

Early in the book, I touched on how often the terms "left wing" and "right wing" signal opposition to the other side. This opposition is sensible to a point because there is a real conflict over the circulation of power. Quite often, however, feelings of antagonism toward the other side become so strong that the focus on opposition overshadows the positions of one's own side. Overwhelmed with animosity for the other side, people lose touch with the positive values that they supposedly support. These people are not so much left-wing or right-wing as they are anti-Right or anti-Left, respectively. These two groups make up most of what people call the "far Left" and the "far Right." These extremist groups are self-defined by negative rather than positive positions.

Horseshoe Theory

First, I need to address a common theory about the far Left and the far Right. The idea of horseshoe theory is that the political spectrum curves back on itself such that the far Left and the far Right of the spectrum converge into the same. The claim is that the far Left and the far Right have far more in common with each other than with the political center.

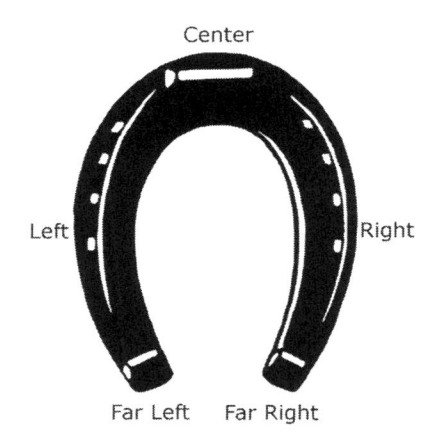

Image in the public domain, author unknown.

 The theory comes from Jean-Pierre Faye who in 2002 attempted to explain how Stalin and Hitler could have agreed to invade and then divide Poland in 1939.[73] Faye created a false dilemma in uncritically adopting the fiction that Stalin was left wing. There is zero reason to think Stalin was in any way left wing. Understanding the right wing as seeking greater concentrations of power places Stalin and his autocratic regime firmly on the absolutist end of the right wing where they belong, alongside Hitler's fascism. There is no fundamental difference between Hitler and Stalin in their use of power, but, more importantly, there is no structural difference in their power. They are both clearly right-wing. There is no need to imagine a horseshoe to explain why they have similar ideologies.

 Horseshoe theory is appealing to those who see themselves as centrists. The center can be portrayed as sensible and of superior quality compared with the alternatives on both extremes. The theory has also been appropriated by conservatives to smear left-wingers as being as bad as the extreme right-wing fascists, if not actually being fascists.

---

[73] Jean-Pierre Faye, *Le Siècle des Idéologies* (Agora, 2002).

Horseshoe theory ignores several obvious facts. One is that the far Left and the far Right oppose each other on policies. They have different visions for society and different goals. The far Right seeks extreme power concentrations, which is exactly what the far Left is trying to destroy. Their conflict is not the same as two right-wing totalitarians fighting for territorial supremacy like Hitler and Stalin did. Again, understanding "left wing" and "right wing" in terms of power concentration resolves confusions about politics. The far Left and the far Right share extremism and maybe even tactics, but that does not mean they are nearly the same as the horseshoe theory implies.

What are the far Left and the far Right? The simple answer would be to say that they are extremes of the left wing and the right wing, but that definition is inadequate. What those who are far Left and far Right have in common is a relative lack of positive values, succumbing as they have to fear of and hatred for those they see as their enemies. The earlier discussion of the right-wing trajectory of reactionism identified its oppositional politics and its reductionist Us-versus-Them view of the world as expressions of a right-wing desire to concentrate power into one's own social group to the exclusion of other social groups.

Perhaps it is the case that an appropriate concentration of power would be good for a society, but far Right groups are not advancing positive solutions. Instead, they are fixated on their antagonism for the supposedly evil left-wingers. Similarly, greater circulation of and inclusion in power are probably good for society, but far Left groups are not advancing positive solutions. Instead, they are fixated on their antagonism for the supposedly evil right-wingers. In their oppositional politics of Us-versus-Them, those commonly thought to be far Left are in practice right-wing, even when they claim to oppose concentrations of power.

Horseshoe theory tries to reflect the shared oppositional politics in both the far Left and the far Right. It is more accurate to think of both groups in terms of their central characteristic—their obsession with opposition. The far Right are the anti-Left—the reactionary right wing that we discussed previously. Opposite the reactionaries are those fixated on opposition to the Right—the anti-Right who are more interested in taking power away from others than in increasing power for anyone. The anti-Right aren't left wing; they are the fake Left.

The Anti-Right Fake Left

The left wing, by definition, is about increasing the circulation of power, increasing the number of people who are included within society and social institutions, and building community. Those positive traits of the Left are not found in the anti-Right, who, being a mirror image of the anti-Left, have perverted anything positive in the left wing into hostile retaliation to anything they see as right-wing. Their hatred of right-wing power structures outweighs any love for their own community. Their opposition is their focus rather than positive action to increase the circulation of power. They claim to be of the Left but think and behave more like the reactionary far Right. They are the fake Left.

The fake Left is characterized by bitterness toward institutions and people who possess power. The feeling comes from an honest place in that excessive concentrations of power are harmful to society, and, historically, most concentrations of power have come about because of abuse and exploitation of others. Certainly, dismantling unjust power structures is essential to increasing the circulation of power and, by extension, justice. However, the fake Left is obsessed with the destruction of power and with their opposition to what they perceive as right-wing institutions. They are more interested in taking power away from other groups than in building power up for the people they say they support.

The fixation with opposition leads the fake Left into contradictory rather than honest responses to abuses of power.

A stunning recent example of this fixation is the fake Left's tacit support for Putin's invasion of Ukraine. They claim to be against war and against imperialism, but when Russian dictator Vladimir Putin started a very clearly imperialist war, the fake Left did not oppose it. Instead, because they are so obsessed with selective opposition, they only repeated their animosity toward the US government and their conspiracy theories that almost everything wrong with the world is caused by the United States. They therefore agreed with Putin's propaganda that placed the blame for Putin's invasion of Ukraine on the United States rather than on Putin.

The authentic left wing is about opposing injustices and increasing power for the oppressed everywhere. The fake Left is not, fixated as they are on opposition and, more to the point, opposition only to particular institutions. They are so anti-Right that they are closed to progress and diversity, and they do not participate in civil discourse about society and power relations. Like the right-wing reactionaries, those of the fake Left tend to see themselves as involved in a culture war rather than in politics. Also like the right-wing reactionaries, those of the fake Left are prone to peddling conspiracy theories of a Them out to get an Us.

The fake Left, fixated on an Us-versus-Them dualism, is closed to mediation and deliberation, especially with the right wing. We must concede that some right-wing arguments in favor of concentrations of power have merit. There are right-wingers who seek power for themselves or seek to deny power to others, but not everyone who pushes for hierarchical power struggles is self-serving. Part of a deliberative democracy is listening to meaningful arguments from all sides and having a constructive dialogue about those ideas. Certainly, those who seek only to silence others and deprive them of power are not engaging in constructive dialogue. We need not accommodate those who use coercion, even when it is clothed in talk of liberty.

The Fake Left Is Anti-Left

The main takeaway from this discussion is that the right-wing reactionaries and the fake Left are locked in opposition to each other rather than engaged in constructive political action. Politics is about community, an idea that goes back to the ancient Greeks; again, the word "politics" comes from the Greek word "polis," meaning the "city community." People on the left wing and the right wing can have different opinions but still all be primarily interested in bettering their community—in seeking the ethical good—and open to dialogue and cooperation. The right-wing reactionaries and the fake Left are not. Theirs is an antipolitics—a drive to divide the community by excluding and otherwise harming others. Ideological extremism moves people outside of politics.

The problem for politics and for society is that the loudest voices are the most heard. Many people are turned off by politics because the political realm has become dominated by the deafening animosity of the right-wing reactionaries and the fake Left. These extremists have so infected political discourse, no doubt helped by social media, that mainstream political parties now engage more in oppositional conflict than in positive politics. It helps to understand that those fixated on opposition are intruding into and trying to stop the political conversation. The right-wing reactionaries and the fake Left are trying to silence other voices and disempower other people. The difficult task for the rest of us is to not let them. We need to continue to try to engage with each other in meaningful dialogue.

Some in the fake Left take their antagonistic approach out of pure hatred. Some others slide into the fake Left out of frustration with the slow rate of progress toward justice or anger over entrenched power structures that favor the right wing and cause harm to others. Siding with the right-wing reactionaries and the fake Left is a dangerous temptation for people willing to submit to simplistic oppositional ideologies because that's easier than the difficult work of constructive politics.

"Keep your eyes on the prize" is great advice for those tempted to give in to anger and vengeance. What is the prize? It is a society in which the circulation of power is not restricted to a select few. It is a society that actively ensures that everyone has enough power to manage their own affairs successfully and that no one has undue power over others. That is the ideal, but it is not idealistic. It is how a healthy human society can be and how most people want it to be.

Appendix 2. The Fake Political Dimension

The traditional conception of the political spectrum, because it doesn't adequately consider the issues of power, has always been inaccurate and confusing. Some have tried to exploit that confusion to push their own agendas, such as the so-called dual-axis political spectrum invented to market political libertarianism. This marketing fake has fooled some people, and because it egregiously misrepresents power relations it needs to be debunked.

The Dual Axis

The dual axis attempts to replace the Left–Right political spectrum by portraying political attitudes on an XY chart. One axis is labeled "left–right" and the other axis reflects some other sentiment, most commonly labeled "authoritarian–libertarian" or "statist–libertarian." My strong tendency as a philosopher is to acknowledge that issues are usually more multidimensional than currently viewed. The dual-axis chart, however, deliberately obfuscates the discussion of political orientation by creating a false dimension.

David Nolan invented the chart in 1969 as a marketing ploy to sell libertarian ideology and the US Libertarian Party that he founded. Nolan set up a diamond-shaped XY chart with one axis suggesting economic freedom and the other axis suggesting personal freedom, which is really social freedom.

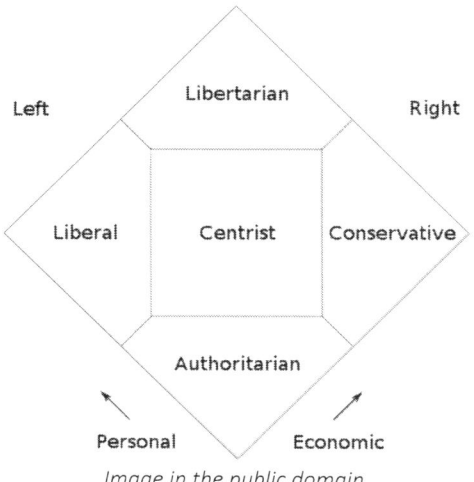

Image in the public domain.

  He placed political libertarianism at the top as though it were divine grace handed down from heaven—a classic marketing technique to put top and center what you want the observer to prefer. Added are the arrows pointing upward to greater freedom, and who wouldn't want greater freedom? The dual-axis diamond, or Nolan Chart, has been used by libertarian groups and political parties as a recruiting tool.

  There are multiple problems with the dual-axis chart, the main one being, as mentioned earlier, its creation of a false dimension. The real-life difference between the left wing and the right wing is their different views on how much concentration of power will achieve the good in society. Nolan's original chart took that grain of truth and oversimplified it into the bromide of "freedom." Then, he artificially split personal and economic freedom into separate axes to obscure the central truth that the Left–Right axis *is* the circulation of power versus the concentration of power. There are various versions based on Nolan's original chart, but they are still variations on these two oversimplifications. As this version indicates, the chart demonizes government.

NOLAN CHART

Libertarian

Government uses force to take property — Less Economic Freedom — Less Personal Freedom — Government uses force to take liberty

Left-wing — More Government use of force — Right-wing

More Personal Freedom — More Economic Freedom

Authoritarian

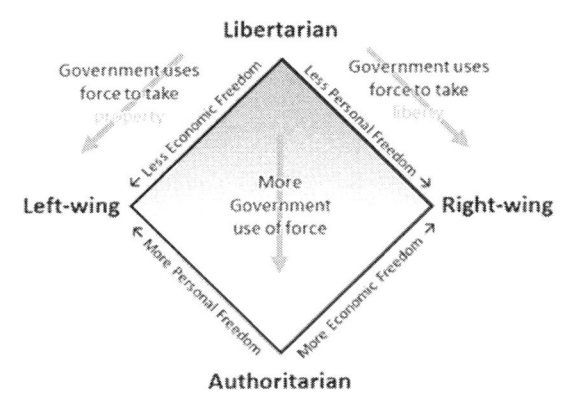

Image in the public domain.

The Dual Axis Debunked

The libertarian dual-axis political spectrum, however construed, quickly collapses under analysis into the single-axis spectrum of concentration of power. The "authoritarian–libertarian" axis *is* the Left–Right axis (although "libertarian" means something other than a greater circulation of liberty, as I will explain). Greater liberty and democratic participation *are* left-wing (liberal)—the increased circulation of power. Greater authoritarianism *is* right-wing (conservative)—the greater concentration of power. It is dishonest to offset liberal and conservative as though they are a different spectrum from the authoritarian–libertarian axis.

Deliberate subterfuge infuses all versions of the libertarian dual-axis chart. The chart is, after all, simply a marketing ploy. In addition to the fabrication of a false dimension, there are three primary areas of subterfuge in the dual axis. One is the artificial separation of economic issues from personal or social issues. The second is the artificial separation of state and private power. The third is masking the complexities of liberty with a false concept of the personal.

The first subterfuge—the false separation of economic and social power—is central to Nolan's original chart and is often copied by followers. It is an attempt to divert attention from the reality that economic power is inextricably intertwined with social power. Granted, the chart does emphasize the libertarian obsession with property rights. Hard power enables soft power, and libertarians know that concentrations of hard power—economic power—lead to concentrations of social power. Their attempt to detach the two is a deliberate distraction from their attempts to concentrate power, as discussed in Chapter 6's section on libertarianism.

The second subterfuge, which is related to the first, is the dual-axis chart's artificial separation of state power concentrations from nonstate power concentrations. Take, for example, this version of the dual-axis chart:

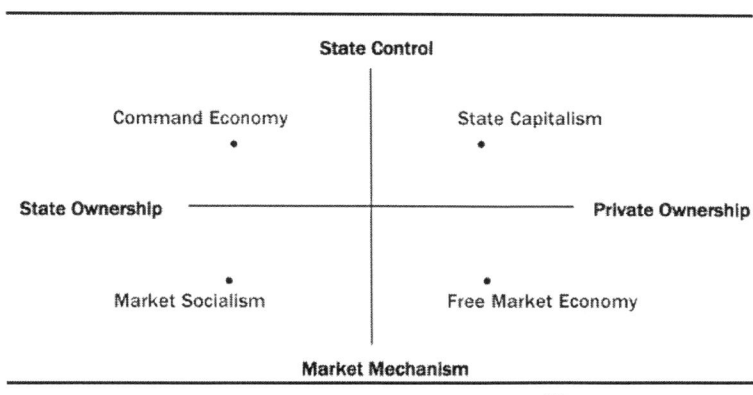

```
                        State Control
                              |
        Command Economy       |      State Capitalism
               •              |            •
                              |
State Ownership ——————————————+—————————————— Private Ownership
                              |
                              |
               •              |            •
        Market Socialism      |      Free Market Economy
                              |
                        Market Mechanism
```

Sujian Guo and Gary Alex Stradiotto.[74]

This version takes Nolan's conflation of economic and personal liberties one step further. Control and ownership have essentially the same outcome, but in an attempt to discredit the concept of the "state," it portrays the "state" as a two-headed evil of control and ownership. Regardless, both "state control" and "state ownership" are the same concentration of power into a single social institution.

---

[74] Sujian Guo and Gary Alex Stradiotto, "The Nature and Direction of Economic Reform in North Korea," *Political Studies* 55(12): 754–778, 2007.

Page | 89

The deliberate subterfuge is using "state" to stand for all concentrations of power. The structure of power relations is what matters, not who or what is at the top of the structure. State control or ownership is a concentration of power and is right-wing, and the same goes for control or ownership by an individual, an aristocracy, or a corporate oligarchy. It is factually misleading and politically dishonest to portray "private ownership" as a panacea in opposition to "state ownership." Both are subject to concentrations of power; both are subject to greater circulation of power. Likewise, "market mechanism" is not a panacea for "state control." When private ownership is excessively concentrated into a few corporations or individuals, they can and will control market mechanisms, as history has shown.

Whether in a small community or a large nation, concentrations of power function similarly. If a small settlement in a dry area has only one source of water that is privately owned, then that individual also has control over that resource. Power is concentrated in that private individual who can leverage that control and ownership to limit the personal and economic freedom of others. If a corporation buys all of the water rights in a region, then the corporation can leverage that concentrated power of control and ownership to limit the personal and economic freedom of others. There is no dichotomy between "state ownership" and "private ownership."

The issue is power concentration. An honest chart about economic control or ownership would have one axis—the Left–Right spectrum reflecting concentration versus circulation of power. The power concentration involves narrowly held control or ownership on one end (right wing) and broadly held control or ownership on the other (left wing). Again, structure is what matters, and all power concentrations function and affect society in fundamentally the same way. An autocrat is an autocrat whether using the label of government or business.

Where Libertarianism Is on the Political Spectrum

Why does the libertarian try to conceal these realities by using the first two subterfuges of the dual-axis chart? What exactly are libertarians who use the chart trying to hide? Political libertarians push the false dimension in the dual-axis spectrum as a sleight-of-hand to try to differentiate their ideology from more familiar right-wing ideologies. Preferring greater power concentration is the definition of right-wing ideology. Again, it does not matter in whom or what the power is concentrated. Libertarians ignore this reality and create the subterfuge that they are outside the Left–Right spectrum and hide that they are, in fact, right-wing. Here is another example of a dual-axis chart that illustrates this:

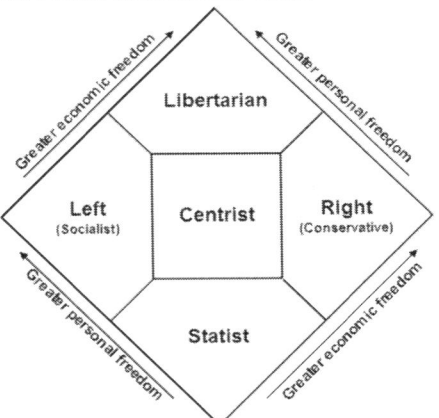

Image in the public domain.

The third subterfuge of the libertarian marketing scheme is to portray liberty as an Absolute Good and pretend that libertarianism is aligned with that sacred Good. Not all forms of "liberty" are a greater circulation of freedom. The dictator has the liberty to take away other people's freedoms. Warlords and gang leaders have the liberty to oppress others. They have these liberties because the structure of power concentration leaves these autocrats free from checks and balances that would stop their oppression of others. There is no rule of law to which coercion and aggression can be held accountable. There is no "state" to enforce laws. It is anarchy—as Hobbes said, the war of all against all.[75]

Political libertarianism's demand for absolute liberty from checks and balances on power inexorably leads to the narrow liberties of the autocrat. Libertarianism is inherently right-wing in its self-serving drive for concentration, not circulation, of "liberty." Part of this subterfuge is relabeling social freedom as "personal" freedom. Libertarianism ignores the reality that the individual is embedded in a world. Libertarians leave society off of their dual-axis chart to hide the fact that other people, not the state, are the biggest constraints on one's personal power. A person can want to do something, but the presence of other people impinges on the freedom to act socially. You can't have that parking space if someone else is already parked there, and abolishing the state won't change that.

Libertarian ideology rests on the mistakes of presuming that governance and accountability to the rule of law are violence and that governance cannot be other than coercion and oppression. This misconception explains why almost all versions of the dual-axis chart portray government or the state as being a negative to overcome. Nolan's original chart set that tone of declaring "the state" as necessarily authoritarian and the worst social structure and libertarianism as the absolute best social structure.

Libertarianism's Right-Wing Fantasy

Political libertarianism is an extreme opposition to government to bring about a particular form of power concentration. The central fallacy of libertarianism is the claim that ending the rule of law—checks and balances on power—would lead to utopia rather than a Hobbesian state of nature.

---

[75] Hobbes, *Leviathan* (Penguin, 2017), 224.

Libertarian ideology considers only negative liberties and demonizes government as the enemy of negative liberties.

It is the child's fantasy of "if there were no rules, I could do whatever I want and I would be happy." Who doesn't want more freedom? But libertarians fundamentally misunderstand the nature of freedom. There are positive freedoms—the ability to do things—and negative freedoms—not being subject to coercion. Libertarians do not understand that freedom is a dynamic among people, and they focus on negative freedoms, such as the perceived tyrannies of governance and legal proscriptions.

Libertarians therefore cannot understand (or willfully ignore) that some restrictions on human behavior are necessary to create more freedom. That is not a paradox. That is the nature of freedom in all aspects of life. Warlords or gang leaders have the liberty to oppress others unless there is a sufficient power to limit their liberty to oppress. Are rules coercion? Sometimes, but rules can, and usually are, in place to bring about greater freedom. Traffic rules allow traffic to flow more freely and safely, and rules only work well if they are obligatory—they cannot be voluntary "if I feel like it." Everyone benefits by not allowing everyone to have the anarchic level of liberty of doing whatever they want without regard to others and shared norms.

Eliminating government will not lead to more freedom. It can lead only to greater tyranny, as can be easily shown. By falsely proclaiming that the governance of the rule of law is coercion and violence, the libertarian claims that all sovereignty should lie in the individual. Society, if it even makes sense to call it that in this context, is then a muddle of individuals disconnected from each other and collective action. In this anarchic situation, the libertarian or anarchist, like a totalitarian leader of a state, is devoid of responsibilities and accountability to others and thus is immune from criticism. The libertarian or anarchist is free to coerce and be violent toward others. It is an empty and false view of freedom—a child's fantasy.

In reality, freedom is a dynamic among people; freedom is never not contingent on other people unless you live in a cave far, far away. (And then your freedom is contingent on the forces of nature.) We live in a shared reality, a society in which cooperation and mutual recognition are essential to freedom. Just as a sporting match requires rules and referees to be a successful and pleasurable game, society needs rules and referees to be able to function for the mutual benefits of people. The presence of other people is inherently a restriction on your liberty. Refusing to acknowledge that you share the world with other people and refusing to negotiate with them guided by a common set of social norms is refusing them their liberty. Life isn't all about you and what you want.

Libertarianism ignores all of these realities in favor of its "if only there were no rules" fantasy: "If only there were no government, I could do whatever I want, and that's liberty." In this way, political libertarianism is extreme right-wing because it would remove all restrictions on and accountability for the use of power, which would inexorably result in a might-makes-right anarchic concentration of power, both economic and social, in the hands of a few who can succeed in overpowering others. Without any social structures to facilitate the circulation of power and limit abuses of power, the libertarian strongmen would have the liberty to be autocratic oppressors.

Marketing political libertarianism in terms of the dual-axis spectrum attempts to hide the truth that political libertarianism is an antisocial anarchism that inexorably leads to totalitarianism. That extreme concentration of power of might makes right is what some libertarians want. Libertarian ideology is right-wing, and its dual-axis marketing scheme is a fundamentally dishonest subterfuge whose intrinsic falsehoods have tricked some people since it was fabricated in 1969. Libertarians have ever since been creating increasingly wacky and overcomplicated versions of the dual-axis chart, each trying to obscure the inherent contradictions of the fake axis that David Nolan created. The real solution is to acknowledge the reality that there is one political spectrum defined by power concentration and that political libertarianism is right-wing, a fact that the dual-axis chart cannot hide.

Forward Foreword

Yes, I'm placing the foreword at the end of the book. That's because my main purpose is to drive political discussion *forward*. Politics is about power; political conflict is about which power concentrations are good or bad. When we put aside the rhetoric of parties and ideologies and engage in deliberative politics about these core issues, when we stop trying to force reality and people into the buttonholes of preconceived ideologies, we have hope for a constructive politics that can build a better society.

A prerelease reviewer of this book remarked that I seemed to lean toward the idea of expanding political power and wondered if this means this book isn't portraying both sides as having equal merit. The reviewer's feedback points to the common practice of thinking of politics in terms of two sides in conflict. The problem is that this viewpoint stifles constructive political conversation. Politics and society at large are far more complex than two sides.

Is there a fundamental conflict between the left wing and the right wing? There are no transcendent entities of Left and Right. There are instead many different people with their many different ways of approaching life and its difficulties. There is no grand historical conflict between the left wing and the right wing, but we can identify "left wing" and "right wing" as different basic approaches to questions of power and human nature.

Do I lean toward the idea of expanding political power? In general, yes, but it's not that simple. As I've previously stated, there are situations in which a greater concentration of power leads to better outcomes. But in the aggregate, increasing the circulation of power in the whole of society leads to better outcomes.

In considering social issues, we need to move away from ideological approaches that interpret situations in terms of fixed agendas. Instead, we need to avoid thinking we know the answers beforehand, be open to exploring and discussing the variables involved, and come to a well-considered answer.

Open exploration and discussion and cooperative decision-making are more possible when power is circulated more. This is perhaps why the prerelease reviewer thought I leaned more to the left wing than to the right wing. Openness to input can be interpreted as a left-wing attitude. Ironically, to want to hear what both right-wingers and left-wingers have to say on an issue is a left-wing, not a right-wing, approach.

A left-wing view of power comes from a fundamentally optimistic view of human nature. Desiring a greater circulation of power is at odds with a pessimistic view of human nature because sharing of power requires mutual trust. The right wing has a fundamentally pessimistic view of human nature. A lack of trust of other people motivates a desire for concentration of power—to deny power to those whom we cannot trust to wield it properly. To be fair, such pessimism is too often justified, as people continually prove. Right-wing methods of coercion and control are quite often excessive, but they are not entirely without reason.

There are many conflicts over power relations. Some are philosophical disputes over what is good for society. Some conflicts are between people who prefer the injustices of power concentrations from which they benefit and people who prefer the justice and freedom that come from greater circulation of power. Those are the many social conflicts between people on the Left and people on the Right who inhabit many degrees along the broad Left–Right political spectrum.

Political action should be based on a sense of reality founded on experience; empathetic understanding of others; sensitivity to the social and political environment; and personal judgment about what is true or untrue, significant or trivial, alterable or unalterable, effective or impractical. Successful political actions that create real benefits will result from dialogue that values openness to mediation of power. We can't please everybody, nor should we try. We can't force the world to bend to our desires, nor should we try. Simplistic answers are simply wrong.

Nevertheless, politicians and influencers continue to offer simplistic answers to complex problems. Rhetoric is easy and so are appeals to fear and loathing. The right wing has the built-in advantages of existing power structures and the reality that blaming others for problems is an easier path than working for change. The right wing also benefits from the fake Left taking that easier path, feeding into the right-wing's Us-versus-Them worldview and culture war mentality rather than working to increase the circulation of power.

Increasing power to the people is a struggle. Working for change is not for the faint of heart. The ideal of a society in which everyone has rights and opportunity is not achieved through wishing it into being or relying on a magic formula. Some wish to believe otherwise, but one cannot just say, "we do this and this and presto, we have liberty and justice!" Reality doesn't work that way, especially social reality. Reality is complex, and nothing is more complex than human society. Simplistic solutions, whether from the right wing or the left wing, ignore reality. Political activism is tough work; people who are into sunshine and unicorns need not apply.

The fruitful path toward the good for society is the rocky and complicated road of circulating power in which we don't give up all of our power to others while we also retain our power to choose from available options and act to effect positive changes in our world. Perhaps foremost in circulating power is to acknowledge that all people are individuals who are capable of thinking for themselves and making their own decisions. The good can come about only by recognizing people as fully human with their own desires and agency.

Bibliography

Berlin, Isaiah. *Four Essays on Liberty*. Oxford University Press, 1969.
Bingham, Tom. *The Rule of Law*. Penguin, 2011.
Burke, Edmund. *Reflections on the Revolution in France*. Oxford University Press, 2009.
Burke, Edmund. "Speech to the Electors of Bristol," *The Works of the Right Honourable Edmund Burke*. ed. Henry G. Bohn, University of Chicago Press. Accessed February 16, 2024, http://press-pubs.uchicago.edu/founders/documents/v1ch13s7.html.
Faye, Jean-Pierre. *Le Siècle des Idéologies*. Agora, 2002.
Federalist Papers: Primary Documents in American History. Library of Congress. https://guides.loc.gov/federalist-papers/text-1-10.
Friedman, David. *The Machinery of Freedom: Guide to a Radical Capitalism*. Chu Hartley, 2014.
Giddens, Anthony. *The Constitution of Society*. Polity, 1984.
Giles, Douglas. *Rethinking Misrecognition and Struggles for Recognition: Critical Theory Beyond Honneth*. Insert Philosophy, 2020.
Green, Thomas Hill. *Prolegomena to Ethics*. Edited by D. Brink. Clarendon Press, 2003.
Guo, Sujian and Stradiotto, Gary Alex. "The Nature and Direction of Economic Reform in North Korea," *Political Studies* 55, No. 12 (2007): 754–778.
Gutmann, Amy and Thompson, Dennis. *Why Deliberative Democracy?* Princeton University Press, 2004.
Habermas, Jürgen. "Hannah Arendt: On the Concept of Power," *Philosophical Political Profiles*. Translated by Frederick G. Lawrence Cambridge, 2012, 171–187.
Han, Byung-Chul. *What Is Power?* John Wiley and Sons, 2018.

Hegel, Georg Wilhelm Friedrich. *Elements of the Philosophy of Right*, edited by Allen W. Wood, translated by H. B. Nisbet. Cambridge University Press, 1991.

Hegel, Georg Wilhelm Friedrich. *Phenomenology of Spirit*. Motilal Banarsidass Publishers, 1998.

Hegel, Georg Wilhelm Friedrich. *Political Writings*, edited by Laurence Dickey and H. B. Nisbet. Cambridge University Press, 1999.

Hobbes, Thomas. *Leviathan*. Penguin, 2017.

Honneth, Axel. *The Struggle for Recognition: The Moral Grammar of Social Conflicts*. Polity, 2003.

Hume, David. *A Treatise of Human Nature*. Penguin, 1986.

Lauritsen, Holger Ross and Thorup, Mikkel (eds.). *Rousseau and Revolution*. Continuum, 2011.

Levitsky, Steven and Ziblatt, Daniel. *How Democracies Die*. Crown, 2018.

Locke, John. *Locke: Two Treatises of Government*. Cambridge University Press, 1988.

Machiavelli, Niccolò. *Discourses on Livy*. Translated by Julia Conaway Bondanella and Peter Bondanella. Oxford University Press, 1997.

Machiavelli, Niccolò. *The Prince*. Translated by George Bull. Penguin, 2003.

Main, Jackson Turner. *The Antifederalists: Critics of the Constitution, 1781–1788*. Omohundro Institute of Early American History and Culture and the University of North Carolina Press, 2017.

Marx, Karl. *Karl Marx: Selected Writings*, 2nd ed., edited by David McLellan. Oxford University Press, 2000.

Mazlish, Bruce. "The Conservative Revolution of Edmund Burke." *The Review of Politics* 20, no. 1 (1958): 21–33.

Mbembe, Achille. *Out of the Dark Night*. Columbia University Press, 2021.

Meierhenrich, Jens and Loughlin, Martin (eds.). *The Cambridge Companion to the Rule of Law*. Cambridge University Press, 2021.

Mill, John Stuart. *On Liberty, Utilitarianism, and Other Essays*. Oxford University Press, 2015.

Mudde, Cas. *Populist Radical Right Parties in Europe.* Cambridge University Press, 2007.

Nozick, Robert. *Anarchy, State, and Utopia.* Blackwell, 1974.

Nye, Joseph S., Jr. "Soft Power: The Evolution of a Concept," *Journal of Political Power*, 14:1, 196–208, 2021.

de Oliveira, Nythamar. "Affirmative Action, Recognition, Self-Respect: Axel Honneth and the Phenomenological Deficit of Critical Theory." In *Justice and Recognition: On Axel Honneth and Critical Theory.* Filosophia and PUCRS, 2015.

O'Neill, Daniel. *Edmund Burke and the Conservative Logic of Empire.* University of California Press, 2016.

Pestritto, Ronald J. and Atto, William J. (eds.). *American Progressivism: A Reader.* Lexington Books, 2008.

Pincus, Steven. *1688: The First Modern Revolution.* Yale University Press, 2009.

Plato. *Republic.* Translated by Desmond Lee. Penguin, 2007.

Popkin, Jeremy D. *A Short History of the French Revolution*, 7th ed., Routledge, 2019.

Rancière, Jacques. *Disagreement: Politics and Philosophy*, Translated by Julie Rose. University of Minnesota Press, 1998.

Rancière, Jacques. *The Ignorant Schoolmaster: Five Lessons in Intellectual Emancipation.* Stanford University Press, 1991.

Robin, Corey. *The Reactionary Mind.* Oxford University Press, 2011.

Rousseau, Jean-Jacques. *Of the Social Contract and Other Political Writings.* Penguin, edited by Christopher Bertram. Translated by Quintin Hoare. Penguin, 2012.

Schmitt, Carl. *Dictatorship.* Translated by Michael Hoelzl and Graham Ward. Polity, 2013.

Schmitt, Carl. *Political Theology.* Translated by George Schwab. University of Chicago Press, 2006.

Made in the USA
Columbia, SC
29 April 2025